FUN IMPROVISATION FOR VIOLIN

The Philosophy and Method of Creative Ability Development
by Alice Kay Kanack

Book 1
Violin

© 1996 Summy-Birchard Music
division of Summy-Birchard Inc.
Exclusive print rights administered by Alfred Publishing Co., Inc.
All Rights Reserved. Printed in USA.

ISBN 0-87487-773-3

cover design: Ernesto Ebanks
art layout: Ken Rehm/Maria A. Chenique

Dedication

To Daphne Jean...
and to all children everywhere, with hope that someday the
world will be a more creative place.

INTRODUCTION

All children are born with creative ability. While it exists innately to varying degrees in every child, it can be developed to a high degree in all children by using a simple formula:

Freedom of Choice

+

Disciplined Practice

=

Creative Ability

Since creativity is essentially the art of making choices a child must be left free to practice making choices (in this case of an artistic musical nature). The freedom of choice is simple to achieve by the complete removal of criticism in the child's creative environment. Thus in CAD the number one rule is "There's No Such Thing As A Mistake!" Freedom from criticism must be paired with disciplined practice in order for the creative process of the brain to develop properly. Like any other ability, the development of creative ability needs lots of practice and repetition.

CAD provides the environmental framework for the student to work within through musical exercises pre-recorded on tape. Instructions are set forth in the guise of games in which there is indeed "no such thing as a mistake." Disciplined practice is achieved through repetition of the games. As the student becomes more accomplished the rules can become more complicated, thus achieving a higher level of creative ability.

The exercises on the tape are based on a theory of how the creative process works in the brain. This theory is introduced and defended in the following chapters. These exercises were tested over a period of ten years by students of the Third Street Music School Settlement with excellent results. These students formed the core of the CAD Tour Group which gave live improvised concerts in the U.S. and abroad. These same students were recognized for their exceptional ability to be uniquely expressive and musical within their regular repertoire as well as while improvising.

Since creativity + music = musicality, it was not surprising that these students developed their expressive abilities to a high degree. Creativity is the art of making choices: Whether those choices are of phrasing or actual notes, the act is essentially the same.

Creativity is also a search: It is an individual's search for truth and beauty within themselves and in the surrounding world. As the student embarks on these exercises remember that he is searching for his best and most sincere solution to the given problem. This search demands the sensitivity and respect of all those in his creative environment.

Table of Contents

PART I

THEORY

THE CREATIVE PROCESS THEORY

CONSCIOUS WORK

Conscious work involves many elements: setting up a problem, repetition of work on the problem, understanding the tools necessary to solve the problem, and exploration of different points of view.

SUBCONSCIOUS WORK

Subconscious work occurs in a part of the brain which we cannot be consciously aware of. It occurs only after conscious work on a creative problem has been attempted repetitiously. It seems to work best when the conscious part of the brain is at rest or is thinking about a subject other than the creative problem at hand. The exact manner in which the subconscious part of the brain functions is the greatest mystery in the creative process.

Some hypothesis are:
1. Heightened Speed and Intensity: It works in a manner similar to our conscious creative searching which is somewhat unique in each person but at a heightened speed and intensity.
2. The Computer: It works like a very complex computer using all information it has been fed by the conscious to find the best or most beautiful solution to the given problem.
3. Natural Shapes of Nature: There are shapes and forms and structures which occur in nature and in our biological systems which, because they are natural, we perceive them as beautiful. As in the "Fibonacci series,' the 'golden mean,' or the 'harmonic series'; these structures which occur in nature in the form of a seashell or the sound of the wind in the trees, may also be part of the way the human brain is structured. Therefore, that structure may become imprinted on the creative ideas fed to the subconscious and result in a more natural, highly structured response which appeals to the human aesthetic concept of beauty.
4. Shapes of the Brain Structure: Creative responses reflect the structure of the brain itself.

INSPIRATION

Inspiration, the highest point in the creative process, occurs when the subconscious having reached a solution to the creative problem, communicates that solution to the conscious. It is characterized by a quality of sudden illumination of thought. It will occur often without warning as a waking dream, complete or nearly complete in form, structure, length, etc. It always occurs in the form of an answer to the problem - not in a theoretical explanation of how that solution was arrived at.

THEORY

Part four in the creative process, is the analysis or theoretical explanation of the inspiration. There is a confusion regarding the correct placement of theory in the creative process because the theories and technical analysis of former inspirations have often been used to begin the creative process on a higher lever. Often the theoretical analysis of a different creative genius will be studied and used by another. In science, mathematics, or medicine it is common to share a thesis on a theoretical basis: In music or art, theories are passed along through the aural/visual study of a particular work. In music, after a period of time theories become written down by theorists whose primary function is to analyze the work of former creative geniuses. These theoretical laws in music, (i.e. the rules of counterpoint, harmony, etc.) can then be studied and broken in music as they are for example in physics when a new inspiration occurs by the next generation of creative geniuses. Because of the breakdown of a central harmonic language in the 20th century, many composers began writing their own harmonic thesis upon which to base their own music. A similar phenomenon occurred in the visual arts in the 20th century. All this served to further confuse the correct placement of theory in the creative process.

A certain amount of rules are necessary to begin a creative process. All creativity is built on creativity. Each new idea grows out of an old one. However, the inspiration is the one truly new creation of the individual which cannot be explained except through the analysis of his work. Therefore, in the creative process this final analysis is actually the only new theoretical work. The theory on which the inspiration had been based, or begun would have been changed, subtly altered or expanded to create a new theory. This new theory, part four of the creative process, could not exist without the inspiration and therefore must follow not precede it.

Further, it is important to recognize that theory is a conscious work process. Theory or analysis, is the conscious working out or explanation of a finished or partially finished creative effort which occurred primarily in the subconscious. This distinction is crucial to the teaching of the creative process. The inspiration can only occur after or during a conscious brain rest or relaxation period. If this conscious relaxation period is not allowed (due to the over-emphasis on theoretical speculation or analysis) the creative effort may be stunted and the inspiration may be blocked.

INSPIRATION, INTUITION, AND INSTINCT

Inspiration, intuition and instinct are all types of subconscious thought process, at least by outward appearances. They share interesting characteristics which may illuminate the workings of the brain.

1. These thought processes are characterized by intense speed. For example, an intuitive sense of danger will occur suddenly, without warning. The instinct to run from danger is strong and fast, leaving no time for conscious thought. Inspiration is the sudden illumination of thought.

2. Inspiration, intuition and instinct (or instinctive reaction) seem to come from an unknown source. Since we cannot be aware of subconscious thought processes except when the subconscious communicates to the conscious, the source (the subconscious) remains a mystery. Therefore, in all three cases it appears that the thought or idea has no internal source.

3. All three occur in answer to an individual's needs. Instinct is an answer to the body's physical needs, inspiration is an answer to an intellectual need, and intuition as we define it is an answer to both physical and intellectual needs.

It appears that these three phenomenon of thought are actually one type of thought process. The separation we give them by calling them instinct, intuition and inspiration refers more to the particular needs they are responding to. It is interesting to note that often human beings (probably because of the mysterious subconscious source) do not trust their instincts, intuitions and inspirations. The lack of understanding regarding these thought processes is likely responsible for the enormous lack of development in this area.

It is interesting that instinct is considered to be a primitive level of thought while evidence here suggests that it may be one of the most complex functions of the brain. If instinct, intuition and inspiration are all derivations and results of a complex subconscious process (which seems logical to assume after considering their shared characteristics), then it is likely that the subconscious functions of the brain have been developing much longer than the conscious functions. Perhaps that is why the subconscious is able to provide solutions which the conscious can only search for.

One of the great challenges of teaching the creative process lies in developing trust in the subconscious. There are two parts to this trust: One is in understanding that each individual has some control over his subconscious; the information which it is given by way of conscious work will in part determine the subconscious response by way of inspiration. Two, one must allow the loss of conscious control over the subconscious. It is not possible to control and one must be relaxed and responsive to the inspiration when it comes since it is the only communication possible between the subconscious and conscious parts of the brain.

MOZART, POINCARÉ AND VAN GOGH

I have read many essays, letters, and accounts regarding the process of creation and have chosen these three to demonstrate the similarities that abound in all of them. Mozart, the supreme musical genius, Poincare the highly regarded mathematician and Van Gogh the revered artist all write in different styles about their particular creative specialty. Yet they are all the same.

In some way they all refer to their disciplined work, their sudden illuminations or inspirations, and their continued development of those inspirations. The key which is so often overlooked in any discussion of the creative process and the teaching of it, is the role that disciplined work plays in achieving inspiration. Inspiration does not merely appear to a gifted fortunate person because he is a gifted fortunate person. Inspiration is earned through hard work. Because throughout history so many great creative geniuses looked at inspiration as a gift (indeed it has the appearance and characteristics of a gift), and did not connect it with their hard work, it has been misunderstood and incorrectly taught for centuries. Inspiration, and the process to achieve it can be taught.

Mozart's *Letter*

When I am, as it were, completely myself, entirely alone, and of good cheer - say, traveling in a carriage, or walking after a good meal, or during the night when I cannot sleep; it is on such occasions that my ideas flow best and most abundantly. Whence and how they come, I know not; nor can I force them. Those ideas that please me I retain in memory, and am accustomed, as I have been told, to hum them to myself. If I continue in this way, it soon occurs to me how I may turn this or that morsel to account, so as to make a good dish of it, that is to say, agreeably to the rules of counterpoint, to the peculiarities of the various instruments, etc.

All this fires my soul, and provided I am not disturbed, my subject enlarges itself, becomes methodized and defined, and the whole, though it be long, stands almost complete and finished in my mind, so that I can survey it, like a fine picture or a beautiful statue, at a glance. Nor do I hear in my imagination the parts successively, but I hear them, as it were, all at once (gleich alles zusammen). What a delight this is I cannot tell! All this inventing, this producing, takes place in a pleasing lively dream. Still the actual hearing of the tout ensemble is after all the best. What has been thus produced I do not easily forget, and this is perhaps the best gift I have my Divine Maker to thank for.

When I proceed to write down my ideas, I take out of the bag of my memory, if I may use that phrase, what has been previously collected into it in the way I have mentioned. For this reason the committing to paper is done quickly enough, for everything is, as I said before, already finished; and it rarely differs on paper from what it was in my imagination. At this occupation I can therefore suffer myself to be disturbed; for whatever may be going on around me, I write, and even talk, but only of fowls and geese, or of Gretel or Barbel, or some such matters. But why my productions take from my hand that particular form and style that makes them Mozartish, and different from the works of other composers, is probably owing to the same cause which renders my nose so large or so aquiline, or in short makes it Mozart's, and different from those of other people. For I really do not study or aim at any originality.

Mozart first writes about inspiration and how it occurs when his conscious mind is in a restful state "after a good meal or during the night." "Whence and how they come, I know not; nor can I force them." The ideas seem to come from somewhere outside himself, a common confusion among artists. It is also interesting to note that inspirations cannot be forced. Mozart is not aware that it is his work which triggers a subconscious process which then becomes conscious. That is why the inspiration often occurs in a restful state: It is easier for the subconscious to communicate to the conscious when the conscious mind is at rest.

Mozart then talks about the work, and here perhaps is part of the key to his genius: Mozart worked on his ideas from memory, never writing down his favorite ideas or working them out on paper. Rather he would "turn this or that morsel to account-agreeably to the rules of counterpoint, to the peculiarities of the various instruments, etc." Mozart did difficult counterpoint and orchestration from memory consciously using these favorite "ideas" or inspirations to create yet another inspiration.

This second inspiration occurs in this description, provided he is "not disturbed" and "stands almost complete and finished in my mind." Nor does Mozart hear "the parts successively" in his mind, he hears them "all at once." In other words, if left alone to allow his mind to focus on the combination of conscious and subconscious work, he can achieve an inspired state in which the total musical work is revealed to him "in a pleasing and lively dream."

He then writes, "What has been thus produced I do not easily forget, and this is perhaps the best gift I have my Divine Maker to thank for." It is interesting that Mozart recognizes his memory as his "best gift" because in a certain sense he is probably correct. The intensity required to consciously work from memory on such difficult tasks as counterpoint, compositional structure and orchestration, is probably why the resulting inspirations are so brilliant. The higher the level of conscious work, the higher the level of subconscious work and inspiration.

Finally the greatest myth about Mozart's creative process is revealed in the final paragraph. He describes how he can sit among friends and write out a fully orchestrated score. As he describes he is simply writing down what he had already created and memorized. The writing of a score from memory is no easy feat, but it has nothing to do with the creative process he previously described. Without the quiet and intense conscious work and resulting inspirations the music could not have been created. Mozart was indeed a genius, but what he did with his gifts of memory and musical ability in the way of difficult disciplined work made him what he was.

Because of Mozart's great brilliance, and his mysterious way of working, a great deal of myth and misunderstanding surrounds the musical creative process. In addition to the analysis of this letter it is important to note that Mozart practiced counterpoint on a daily basis from the time he was a child. Counterpoint is a very strict form of composition using two or more parts simultaneously to create a piece of music. This form of composition has strict rules which require much thought and concentration. It is also important to note that Mozart was recognized in his day as a great improviser. Improvisation is an art in which the musician creates music spontaneously. Mozart was famous for doing this as a soloist and also with an orchestra. His piano concertos were often written only as a skeleton which he would fill in as he performed. We are therefore left with a great many incomplete written works by Mozart. The role of improvisation in the creative process will be discussed at length in another chapter.

Excerpts from *Mathematical Creation* by Poincaré

It is time to penetrate deeper and to see what goes on in the very soul of the mathematician. For this, I believe, I can do best by recalling memories of my own. But I shall limit myself to telling how I wrote my first memoir on Fuchsian functions. I beg the reader's pardon; I am about to use some technical expressions, but they need not frighten him, for he is not obliged to understand them. I shall say, for example, that I have found the demonstration of such a theorem under such circumstances. This theorem will have a barbarous name, unfamiliar to many, but that is unimportant; what is of interest for the psychologist is not the theorem but the circumstances.

For fifteen days I strove to prove that there could not be any functions like those I have since called Fuchsian functions. I was then very ignorant; every day I seated myself at my work table, stayed an hour or two, tried a great number of combinations and reached no results. One evening, contrary to my custom, I drank black coffee and could not sleep. Ideas rose in crowds; I felt them collide until pairs interlocked, so to speak, making a stable combination. By the next morning I had established the existence of a class of Fuchsian functions, those which come from the hypergeometric series; I had only to write out the results, which took but a few hours.

Then I wanted to represent these functions by the quotient of two series; this idea was perfectly conscious and deliberate, the analogy with elliptic functions guided me. I asked myself what properties these series must have if they existed, and I succeeded without difficulty in forming the series I have called theta-Fuchsian.

Just at this time I left Caen, where I was then living, to go on a geologic excursion under the auspices of the school of mines. The changes of travel made me forget my mathematical work. Having reached Coutances, we entered an omnibus to go some place or other. At the moment when I put my foot on the step the idea came to me, without anything in my former thoughts seeming to have paved the way for it, that the transformations I had used to define the Fuchsian functions were identical with those of non-Euclidean geometry. I did not verify the idea; I should not have had time, as, upon taking my seat in the omnibus, I went on with a conversation already commenced, but I felt a perfect certainty. On my return to Caen, for conscience's sake I verified the result at my leisure.

Then I turned my attention to the study of some arithmetical questions apparently without much success and without a suspicion of any connection with my preceding researches. Disgusted with my failure, I went to spend a few days at the seaside, and thought of something else. One morning, walking on the bluff, the idea came to me, with just the same characteristics of brevity, suddenness and immediate certainty, that the arithmetic transformations of indeterminate ternary quadratic forms were identical with those of non-Euclidean geometry.

Returned to Caen, I meditated on this result and deduced the consequences. The example of quadratic forms showed me that there were Fuchsian groups other than those corresponding to the hypergeometric series; I saw that I could apply to them the theory of theta-Fuchsian series and that consequently there existed Fuchsian functions other than those from the hypergeometric series, the ones I then knew. Naturally I set myself to form all these functions. I made a systematic attack upon them and carried all the outworks, one after another. There was one however that still held out, whose fall would involve that of the whole place. But all my efforts only served at first the better to show me the difficulty, which indeed was something. All this work was perfectly conscious.

Thereupon I left for Mont-Valerien, where I was to go through my military service; so I was very differently occupied. One day, going along the street, the solution of the difficulty which had stopped me suddenly appeared to me. I did not try to go deep into it immediately, and only after my service did I again take up the question. I had all the elements and had only to arrange them and put them together. So I wrote out my final memoir at a single stroke and without difficulty.

I shall limit myself to this single example; it is useless to multiply them. In regard to my other researches I would have to say analogous things, and the observations of other mathematicians given in L'Enseignement Mathematique would only confirm them.

Most striking at first is this appearance of sudden illumination, a manifest sign of long, unconscious prior work. The role of this unconscious work in mathematical invention appears to me incontestable, and traces of it would be found in other cases where it is less evident. Often when one works at a hard question, nothing good is accomplished at the first attack. Then one takes a rest, longer or shorter, and sits down anew to the work. During the first half-hour, as before, nothing is found, and then all of a sudden the decisive idea presents itself to the mind. It might be said that the conscious work has been more fruitful because it has been interrupted and the rest has given back to the mind its force and freshness. But it is more probable that this rest has been filled out with unconscious work and that the result of this work has afterward revealed itself to the geometer just as in the cases I have cited; only the revelation, instead of coming during a walk or a journey, has happened during a period of conscious work, but independently of this work which plays at most a role of excitant, as if it were the goad stimulating the results already reached during rest, but remaining unconscious, to assume the conscious form.

There is another remark to be made about the conditions of this unconscious work: it is possible, and of a certainty it is only fruitful, if it is on the one hand preceded and on the other hand followed by a period of conscious work. These sudden inspirations (and the examples already cited sufficiently prove this) never happen except after some days of voluntary effort which has appeared absolutely fruitless and whence nothing good seems to have come, where the way taken seems totally astray. These efforts then have not been as sterile as one things; they have set agoing the unconscious machine and without them it would not have moved and would have produced nothing.

The need for the second period of conscious work, after the inspiration, is still easier to understand. It is necessary to put in shape the results of this inspiration, to deduce from them the immediate consequences, to arrange them, to word the demonstrations, but above all is verification necessary. I have spoken of the feeling of absolute certitude accompanying the inspiration; in the cases cited this feeling was no deceiver, nor is it usually. But do not think this is a rule without exception; often this feeling deceives us without being any the less vivid, and we only find it out when we seek to put on foot the demonstration. I have especially noticed this fact in regard to ideas coming to me in the morning or evening in bed while in a semi-hypnagogic state.

Such are the realities; now for the thoughts they force upon us. The unconscious, or, as we say, the subliminal self plays an important role in mathematical creation; this follows from what we have said. But usually the subliminal self is considered as purely automatic. Now we have seen that mathematical work is not simply mechanical, that it could not be done by a machine, however perfect. It is not merely a question of applying rules, or making the most combinations possible according to certain fixed laws. The combinations so obtained would be exceedingly numerous, useless and cumbersome. The true work of the inventor consists in choosing among these combinations so as to eliminate the useless ones or rather to avoid the trouble of making them, and the rules which must guide this choice are extremely fine and delicate. It is almost impossible to state them precisely; they are felt rather than formulated. Under these conditions, how imagine a sieve capable of applying them mechanically?

A first hypothesis now presents itself: the subliminal self is in no way inferior to the conscious self; it is not purely automatic; it is capable of discernment; it has tact, delicacy; it knows how to choose, to divine. What do I say? It knows better how to divine than the conscious self, since it succeeds where that has failed. In a word, is not the subliminal self superior to the conscious self? You recognize the full importance of this question. Boutroux in a recent lecture has shown how it came up on a very different occasion, and what consequences would follow an affirmative answer.

Is this affirmative answer forced upon us by the facts I have just given? I confess that, for my part, I should hate to accept it. Reexamine the facts then and see if they are not compatible with another explanation.

It is certain that the combinations which present themselves to the mind in a sort of sudden illumination, after an unconscious working somewhat prolonged, are generally useful and fertile combinations, which seem the result of a first impression. Does it follow that the subliminal self, having divined by a delicate intuition that these combinations would be useful, has formed only these, or has it rather formed many others which were lacking in interest and have remained unconscious?

In this second way of looking at it, all the combinations would be formed in consequence of the automatism of the subliminal self, but only the interesting ones would break into the domain of consciousness. And this is still very mysterious. What is the cause that, among the thousand products of our unconscious activity, some are called to pass the threshold, while others remain below? Is it a simple chance which confers to this privilege? Evidently not; among all the stimuli of our senses, for example, only the most intense fix our attention, unless it has been drawn to them by other causes. More generally the privileged unconscious phenomena, those susceptible of becoming conscious, are those which, directly or indirectly, affect most profoundly our emotional sensibility.

It may be surprising to see emotional sensibility invoked a propos of mathematical demonstrations which, it would seem, can interest only the intellect. This would be to forget the feeling of mathematical beauty, of the harmony of numbers and forms, of geometric elegance. This is a true esthetic feeling that all real mathematicians know, and surely it belongs to emotional sensibility.

Now, what are the mathematic entities to which we attribute this character of beauty and elegance, and which are capable of developing in us a sort of esthetic emotion? They are those whose elements are harmoniously disposed so that the mind without effort can embrace their totality while realizing the details. This harmony is at once a satisfaction of our esthetic needs and an aid to the mind, sustaining and guiding. And at the same time, in putting under our eyes a well-ordered whole, it makes us foresee a mathematical law. Now, as we have said above, the only mathematical facts worthy of fixing our attention and capable of being useful are those which can teach us a mathematical law. So that we reach the following conclusion: The useful combinations are precisely the most beautiful, I mean those best able to charm this special sensibility that all mathematicians know, but of which the profane are so ignorant as often to be tempted to smile at it.

Translated by George Bruce Halsted
"Mathematical Creation" from The Foundations of Science.

Poincaré's Mathematical Creation, so elegant and precise, needs very little explanation. Rather it should be read and highlighted for its clarity of vision in the area of the creative process. I include it here because it was an invaluable resource in the development of my theory and method. I also include it because it dispels a great falsehood in the realm of medical, mathematical and scientific research: That the creative process is somehow different for scientists and mathematicians than it is for artists and musicians. It is not. (Poincaré not only shows how it is the same, but clearly indicates the process in scientific and artistic terms.)

Beginning with Poincaré's description of the discovery of Fuchsian functions, one can immediately see the relationship between his creative process and Mozart's. First came the initial inspiration - in this case, an idea that there "could not be any functions like those I have since called Fuchsian functions." This idea would be equal to Mozart's first melodic ideas. Every day for fifteen days Poincaré continued to consciously work on this idea with no result; a parallel to Mozart's working out of counterpoint and orchestration in his conscious mind. Then came the inspiration. It is interesting that Mozart and Poincaré both describe the event taking place at night in an almost woken dream state. A state in which the conscious mind is resting and the subconscious is breaking through to cause a sleepy agitation. Compare "All this fires my soul - My subject enlarges itself, becomes methodized and defined, and the whole, though it be long, stands almost complete and finished in my mind - All this inventing - takes place in a pleasing lively dream." Mozart. / "One evening - I could not sleep. Ideas rose in crowds; I felt them collide until pairs interlocked, so to speak, making a stable combination. By the next morning I had established the existence of a class of Fuchsian functions - I had only to write out the results, which took but a few hours." Poincaré.

Poincaré goes on to describe further conscious work, inspirations and theoretical working out of his final memoir on Fuchsian functions always noting the differences in the way his brain worked on the problem. Using this as an example, Poincaré describes what he believes occurs in the brain during the creative process. He recognizes, as I do in the analysis of Mozart's letter, that inspirations "never happen except after some days of voluntary effort." He also recognizes the existence of what he calls the "unconscious machine," what I call the subconscious process, and its role in creating inspirations. He further states the need of "verification" because the inspiration occurs as a complete or nearly complete solution which, especially in the areas of science, math or medicine, need to be explained and proven theoretically. Particularly because an inspiration may prove to be a false solution to the particular problem at hand.

This idea fascinated me when I first read it because I, like many people think of science, math or medicine as exact entities. Ones which require a great deal of knowledge and theoretical work. I incorrectly assumed that inspiration was limited to the arts, and if ideas occurred to scientists they came through the conscious working out of theoretical problems or hypothesis. The idea that inspiration in the scientific realm occurs in such mass proportions, and that major discoveries occurred through inspiration and were followed by theoretical analysis was exciting. Exciting because I realized that this same creative process which I was coming to understand could be taught through the arts and sciences and since they were essentially the same process there could be a lot of carry over into all fields of study.

There is another area which Poincaré writes about which is shared by the creative processes of arts and sciences: The role of beauty in the subconscious process. In the beginning of the book I stated that creative ability is the search for truth and beauty. It is easy to see how truth is the primary goal in the scientific creative processes, but it surprised me to read what Poincaré had to say about "mathematical beauty," "the harmony of numbers and forms" and "geometric elegance." He writes that it is possible that this beauty guides the researcher to mathematical law because "The useful combinations are precisely the most beautiful, I mean those best able to charm this special sensibility that all mathematicians know, but of which the profane are so ignorant as often to be tempted to smile at it." He describes how this mathematical beauty satisfies "aesthetic needs" in the scientist thereby "guiding and sustaining" his journey towards the truth. (I believe these aesthetic needs exist in all people and begin to manifest themselves in children about the age of two.)

Vincent van Gogh: *Excerpt from a letter to Anton Ridder Van Rappard*

When I have a model who is quiet and steady and with whom I am acquainted, then I draw repeatedly till there is one drawing that is different from the rest, which does not look like an ordinary study, but more typical and with more feeling. All the same it was made under circumstances similar to those of the others, yet the latter are just studies with less feeling and life in them. This manner of working is like another one, just as plausible. As to The Little Winter Gardens, for example, you said yourself they had so much feeling; all right, but that was not accidental - I drew them several times and there was no feeling in them. Then afterwards - after I had done the ones that were so stiff - came the others. It is the same with the clumsy and awkward things. HOW IT HAPPENS THAT I CAN EXPRESS SOMETHING OF THAT KIND? Because the thing has already taken form in my mind before I start on it. The first attempts are absolutely unbearable. I say this because I want you to know that if you see something worthwhile in what I am doing, it is not by accident but because of real intention and purpose.

> Translated by Rela van Messel
> from *Letters to an Artist:*
> *Vincent van Gogh to Anton Ridder van Rappard.*

Once again we see the pattern: One, the initial inspiration "the thing has already taken form in my mind before I start on it." Two, the conscious work, "I draw repeatedly" and Three, the inspiration "Then afterwards - after I had done the ones that were so stiff - came the others" different from the rest more typical and with more feeling.

The repeated drawing is like a form of artistic improvisation similar to Mozart's musical one. Both perhaps based on a predetermined form, but not necessarily so. It is interesting to note that while Van Gogh has an initial inspiration, he is not able to instantly reproduce it on canvas, rather he finds it necessary to do the physical improvisations and wait for it to change on the paper. It's almost as if his subconscious needs to reach his hands after it has reached his conscious brain.

Van Gogh, Mozart and Poincaré are three very different creative geniuses. As you have seen however, their creative processes are essentially the same. There are many others: Picasso, Mary Wigman, D.H. Lawrence, Henry Moore, Jean Cocteau, Einstein, William Wordsworth, etc. whose writings on the creative process all agree with this pattern which has been described. In order to develop a method for teaching the creative process I first wrote my theory of the creative process based on these and other writings.

I believe this theory of the creative thought process has existed for hundreds, maybe even thousands of years, and yet it has never been written down with the idea of developing a method by which young children could learn about it, and also learn how to use it towards their own individual creative ends. The evidence of the existence of the subconscious process is strong in these writings, and though, as yet unproven in studies of the brain, evidence suggested by students studying CAD (the method based on these theories) is even stronger. All students reach the point of inspiration after two to three years in the program and some of the more advanced students have achieved the "double" inspirations as documented by Poincaré, Mozart and Van Gogh.

LESSONS WITH JOSEPH SCHWANTNER

Joseph Schwantner, the Pulitzer Prize winning composer, was my first composition teacher at Eastman. We agreed that my first assignment would be a simple one; a song for voice and piano. The writing of this song taught me valuable lessons about the art of composition and inspiration.

The first week I wrote a song and brought it in to my lesson. Schwantner did not criticize it. Instead he asked me to write four different harmonizations of the song so that we could choose the best one. For the remainder of the lesson he showed me scores by other composers and we listened to music.

For the next several weeks I brought in different harmonziations and arrangements of the same song. Each time, Schwantner would ask me for more, and again play me more music and show me more scores by other composers. As the weeks went by I became more and more frustrated and found that I liked the piece less and less. I knew that it was better than when I started, but I also knew that it wasn't having the power that I wanted.

Finally, the week before my last lesson before the Christmas holiday, it all came to a head. I was working late one night in a practice room and finally became so frustrated that I picked up the music, tore it up, and threw it away. Suddenly ideas, inspirations, started flowing, It was the song but not the song. It was a completely new arrangement of the song, keeping the parts I liked best and replacing other parts with much better music. I quickly began writing and within the hour I had the work complete.

I brought this song to my lesson and Schwantner said "That's it. The song is finished." I couldn't believe it. How did he know? I told him what had happened and he just smiled and put on some new music to listen to.

To this day I wonder how he knew, though I now understand it much better. It was like the example Van Gogh spoke of. He drew and drew until there was one with more feeling, more depth than all the rest. Schwantner was able to see this when it happened to my song.

Today when I listen to my CAD students I can tell when their performances and pieces are inspired and when they are not. Again it is this feeling of greater emotional power and beauty. This quality appears in both a child's creation and in his performance.

There was more in this lesson than the recognition of inspiration. There were the ingredients that made it happen:

1. Repetition of a question or problem needing a solution. Like Poincaré's Fuchsian functions, or Van Gogh's painting, or my song. The exercise was repeated until it produced a significant inspired reaction.

2. There was no criticism from Schwantner at any time during the creative process. If he had criticized the song I would have been searching, not to find my best solution, but to find his. In a sense he would have become the composer through me. While there is great value in the study of other composers and their music, their styles should never be forced upon a work in progress. This would be stifling. The criticism of an original composition, particularly one in progress, is a very painful experience because original music comes from the composer's unique sensitivity to truth and beauty. No two people are exactly alike in their artistic senses. Schwantner understood this.

3. I was exposed to a great deal of music which I had never heard before. Remember at each lesson Schwantner showed me scores and played music for me. Much of it was very beautiful and impressionable. In this way, I was given many styles and ideas to choose from in my own composition. I learned about form, structure, harmony, arrangement, orchestration, etc. from these composers that Schwantner played for me. As I worked, this music was introduced to my subconscious process along with my specific ideas for my song. When I became inspired these ideas blended together to create my original use of what I had learned. Creativity is built on creativity. Each new idea comes out of an old one and is built upon it.

4. By throwing away the written song I was able to tap into the subconscious and become inspired. I had forced the focus of my brain on the written page and blocked the subconscious up to that point. The

removal of that block and the resting of my conscious allowed the inspiration to break through. It is very important to work in such a way as to allow this communication of subconscious and conscious, and to also teach the conscious to listen.

THE TWO MYSTERIES OF CREATIVE ABILITY

Throughout history, the ability to be creative has been largely ignored in educational circles. There are two reasons for this which I call the two mysteries of creative ability: One, the mystery of the correct nature and explanation of inspiration and two, the seemingly contradictory roles freedom and discipline play in the creative process. Because of these mysteries most educators decided that creative ability was unteachable. They felt (as most people still do today) that creative children would develop their creative abilities on their own without help or interference, and non-creative children would not develop creative abilities regardless of educational opportunities. Creative ability has come to be regarded as something one is either born with or born without, rather like musical talent was believed to be until Shinichi Suzuki began his talent education method in the 1940's. Suzuki has clearly demonstrated that musical talent belongs to all children if their musical ability is developed properly from an early age. Suzuki, who also uses the name "mother tongue" to describe his method, shows how musical ability can be developed in the same way that children learn to speak their native language between the ages of 0-5. CAD claims that creative ability, like linguistic or musical abilities, exists in all children and can be developed to a very high level given proper training. This idea is clearly at odds with beliefs held by most educators. The unraveling of the two mysteries will clarify the reasons for this disparity.

Mystery #1: Freedom vs. Discipline

Freedom has always been associated with creativity. In order to be creative one needs a great deal of freedom. The question is what kind of freedom? Some experimental educators in attempting to encourage greater creative ability, gave children complete freedom with disastrous results. What they failed to realize was that freedom and discipline are not opposites in education. In combination, a certain type of freedom and a certain type of discipline make - up the perfect formula for developing creative ability.

The formula is:

Freedom of Choice

or

Freedom from criticism

+

Disciplined practice and repetition of making choices

=

Creative Ability

Freedom of choice is necessary because creativity is essentially the art of making choices. Choices of good or bad, beautiful or ugly, right or wrong, are how an artist or scientist creates their own unique perspective. Through choices the creator defines his work as his own. If a teacher, parent, or fellow student criticizes a creator's choices that person becomes the creator by virtue of his criticism. That criticism is that person's choice of the correct solution to the given creative problem. Therefore, in order for each individual to develop his own creative ability he must be free to make his own choices without any interruption or criticism.

Discipline is also necessary. Repetition of conscious work on a given problem triggers the subconscious to come up with a greater more complete solution to that problem. Without this disciplined work the subconscious will not become involved and will not develop. Of course, the conscious process will not develop either.

Opposite of the common misconception, there is no such thing as a great creative genius who does not (or did not) work with great discipline and tons of repetition.

Therefore, the title of this section, "Freedom vs. Discipline," has one problem: The "vs." needs to be replaced with a "+" so that it reads "Freedom + Discipline." It is this small word that is needed to clarify and solve this mystery.

Mystery #2: Inspiration

Inspiration, or more specifically where it comes from, is the basis of mystery #2. Inspiration is the result of the conscious mind working on a problem which is then taken over by the subconscious. The subconscious solution to the problem is presented to the conscious by means of the inspiration: A sudden "illuminating" thought which contains the complete or partially complete solution to the creative problem being worked on.

The fact that the inspiration is the result of a subconscious process is the basis of the mystery. Since we cannot witness the subconscious process except for its end result, we tend to give credit to a power outside of ourselves, i.e. God. Throughout history creative geniuses in all fields gave credit to God for their inspirations, failing to recognize that it was their hard work which triggered the inspired thoughts. Indeed there are several definitions of the word inspired in the dictionary one of which is "2: To influence, move or guide by divine or supernatural inspiration" or another "5: to communicate to an agent supernaturally; also: Create."

The idea that inspiration is a gift from God is not a surprising one, given the qualities of sudden perfection, beauty and emotional power that usually accompany an inspiration. The fact that the inspiration usually uncovers a truth that the conscious was searching for (without success) is another powerful indication of a Godlike presence in an inspiration.

But, whether one believes in a God or not the evidence is strong to support the idea that inspiration comes from within the human brain, and can only be triggered by conscious repetitious work on a creative problem. We have been given the gift of a brain, how we use and develop it is up to us.

The idea of inspiration being a gift leads to an attitude of hopelessness regarding one's ability to achieve one. This leads to lack of work and development towards the highest point in the creative process: Inspiration.

THE 80/20 SYNDROME

Though every child is born with creative ability, his ability to use it in relation to other skills varies from child to child. The creative thought process is distinctly different from other thought processes and is apparent in different ratios in different children. Just as the lobes of the brain are asymmetrical, the balance of abilities is different in every child.

A good analogy to innate balances in the brain is the innate balance of the right and left hand. Some children are born right-handed, others are born left-handed. Suppose for a moment all the children went to school and had their right hands tied behind their backs. They were then asked to do tasks with their left hands and judged on their abilities accordingly. Of course the left-handed children would do very well, appear coordinated and demonstrate strong ability, while the right-handed children would appear slow, uncoordinated and incapable of even the simplest tasks. This would obviously be an inaccurate assessment of these children.

Unfortunately this example is precisely what happens to creative children in a typical non-creative school environment. Not only are their stronger abilities not developed, they are actually ignored, sometimes ridiculed, basically "tied behind their backs."

This is ignoring an even more crucial point: The hands work together. Whether a child is left or right handed he uses his weaker hand to help his stronger hand and vice versa. The thought processes of the brain work in exactly the same way. Development of all types of thought processes will result in the highest level of ability being achieved by each child.

In my work I have noted two distinctly different types of thought processes which occur in children: The creative thought process and the analytical thought process. Unfortunately the child with a dominantly creative thought process can often be identified by his struggles in a predominantly analytical skills environment. He has difficulty with coordination, memorization, and basic logical skills. However, give this child a creative problem to solve and he will do it brilliantly and with ease.

The child with the dominantly analytical thought process excels in logical, analytical and memorization skills. He is often a straight A student, but when faced with a creative problem he will attempt to avoid it or struggle with it, never solving it to his complete satisfaction.

Most children have both of these thought processes in a ratio of 60:40 or 40:60, one being slightly more creative or slightly more analytical in their thought process. More rarely is the occurrence of an 80:20 or 20:80 child. CAD was born out of a chance encounter with just such a child.

Daniel was 80:20, predominantly creative but without any outlet for his ability. After one year of violin study in the fifth grade he was terribly uncoordinated, unfocused, out of tune and unable to grasp the rudiments of note reading. I was called on to tutor him and soon found traditional note reading exercises to be completely useless with this child. I decided after much thought, to approach the reading problem from a different angle. My plan was to help him create his own music, then write it down, and by these means help him to read. The experiment was an enormous success. In his lesson the first week I gave him a basic improvisation exercise: I asked him to play anything he wanted to using a simple finger pattern while I improvised on the piano. He immediately became focused, coordinated, and played in tune; but what was more startling was the beautiful music that poured from his heart into his violin. In the following lessons he continued to create, learned to read and learned to compose beautifully. His ability to learn pieces and technique during this period also dramatically improved. My experience with this student made me aware of the enormous hole in our educational system: One which could let an enormously talented child appear inadequate.

Whether a child is predominantly creative or non-creative he still needs the benefits of exercising his creative thought process though for different reasons.

Why Creative Children Need CAD

History is full of stories about creative geniuses who did badly in school as youngsters (Einstein, Edison, etc.). Our education system is based on what can be taught through memorization, logic and reason - all strictly conscious functions of the brain, all type II children (with the analytical thought process style learning). The creative child is lost in this environment, the more extreme his creative side the more lost this child is. Without an outlet and guidance this child cannot use his terrific natural creative ability to help himself learn. His confidence is low and he is probably frustrated and bored.

Daniel was a creative child of the extreme kind. CAD was very helpful to him in releasing and directing his creative ability. It also helped him to read music and write music and to have better physical control of his instrument. Since Daniel, I have seen several other children of this type. They flourish in CAD class, where they express themselves with power and emotion. They move quickly to higher levels - and need constant creative challenges so they are not bored.

Through the redirection of energy and natural ability these children are better able to deal with memorization and coordination exercises. They are also better able to correct weaknesses in their musical language such as pitch and rhythmic accuracy. I have witnessed startling cases in which previously nearly tone deaf children could correct their deficiencies to the point where they appeared to have above average to excellent proficiency in this difficult area of pitch recognition and reproduction.

This evidence suggests that these students were able to use the creative thought process to develop skills which were unrelated to the process itself. Just as some children are able to use conscious analytical thought processes to solve problems or difficulties (weaknesses) in their learning of tools and information, other children are able to use the creative thought process to achieve the same goals. The creative thought process can act as an illuminator or catalyst to information or activities other than the creative process at hand.

Why Non-Creative Children Need CAD

Non-creative children or children with a stronger analytical memorization skills side need to develop their creative ability because it is weaker. Creative ability is half of the development of any type of intelligence. For example, musicians who can learn music, memorize it, imitate other interpretations and perform are not great artists. They are not great artists because they lack the crucial ingredient: creative ability. In musical performance, creative ability manifests itself as what is commonly called musicality: (the ability to interpret and express emotion, direction and content in a piece of music). The ability to make original choices of an aesthetic nature and perform those choices is a creative ability. An artist is one who has both great technical proficiency and great creative ability (or great original musicality). A non-creative child, without development of his weaker side, will be unable to become an artist, he will be merely an imitative technically proficient musician.

PART II

HOW TO DEVELOP YOUR CHILD'S CREATIVE ABILITY

HOW CREATIVE ABILITY IS DESTROYED

Creative ability is extremely easy to destroy. Most of the destruction is unintentional, caused by a parent's lack of knowledge regarding the initial appearance of creative ability in a child. There are very few parents who would not love to encourage every talent or ability their children demonstrate, but because they don't understand these initial artistic expressions parents are most often responsible for the destruction of them.

Here are some examples:
1. "Stop banging on the piano"
2. "Try to draw between the lines"
3. "What is that a picture of?"

Children often begin their creative musical expression with their voices. Children love to sing or hum while they're playing games. A young child, confronted by a piano will almost always be drawn to explore it. At this age, 2-5, a child's small muscle control will be undeveloped and so he will at first use palms rather than fingers to make sounds. Thus, the banging sound and the parent's response "stop banging on the piano." The child will then be quickly discouraged from further creative exploration. If left alone to explore the child would eventually develop that muscle control and would probably begin creating melodies. If the child were encouraged to explore through musical games, his development would increase rapidly and his ability would dramatically improve.

A good comparison is to language. A baby makes sounds, "gaga, googoo," etc., before he says his first word. Those sounds are responded to by his mother and father with love and comfort. When he says his first word "mama, papa" etc., there is a great celebration and more love and comfort. His basic needs are answered whenever he speaks. Now, just suppose that, rather than love and attention, the baby's first sounds and words were greeted with angry shouts or that he was put away in a room by himself and ignored. That child's development would be severely stunted and he might have great difficulty learning to speak. Fortunately, most parents respond to their babies the first way and most children learn to speak beautifully by the age of five. Unfortunately most parents respond the opposite way to initial artistic expressions, ignoring or criticizing these crucial first steps.

It is clear that the reasons for this stem from certain myths of creative genius. We all know that Mozart was a child prodigy. What most people don't realize is that nobody plays Mozart's early music. Why? Because it isn't very good! Mozart's early expressions were childlike. He probably even started with a few bangs like most children. Somehow people came to believe that if their child didn't immediately play beautiful melodies and harmonies, that child was without creative musical ability. That's like saying, "if my baby doesn't create a Shakespeare-like sonnet with his first words he'll never be a poet." Of course, we all know that's ludicrous.

Drawing is the same. Often a child's first drawings are unrecognizable to adults (just like his first words or sounds). They are crude or rough because the child cannot control his movements very well. Also, the perspective of a child is different from that of an adult. Confronted by a drawing by a child the adult will often respond "what is that a picture of?" The child is hurt by the adult's failure to see what he sees and is easily discouraged. Mendelowitz suggests a better question would be "Can you tell me about it?" This will encourage the child to talk about the picture and will reward his effort to communicate artistically with the adult. Again, the first drawing will not look like a Renoir or a Picasso or a Van Gogh.

"Try to draw between the lines" is a misguided effort to control the speed at which a child develops artistically. Drawing between the lines is fine if one wants to develop the child's ability to draw between lines (or in other words control the motions of his hands). As an artistic aid it must fail because in essence it is doing the opposite. It is removing the child's freedom to choose what he wishes to draw and how he wishes to draw it. As we have said before 'Freedom of choice' is one of the primary ingredients in developing creative ability. Further, telling a child to 'draw between the lines' is suggesting to him that this kind of drawing is more correct or appropriate than his explorations outside the lines or on a blank piece of paper. We have therefore also removed 'Freedom from criticism,' another primary ingredient in the development of creative ability.

Destruction of creative ability is so easy and parents aren't the only ones responsible. Teachers and other children are equally destructive. Criticism, humor at a child's expense, and neglect are all ways of destruction that are unfortunately all too common. Again, these destructive items are often the result of misinformation about the myths of creative genius. Rarely are they a direct attempt to ridicule or stunt the creative growth of a child.

Destruction is so easy because of the nature of creativity. The creative act is a deeply personal expression of the child's unique view of beauty and truth. That personal view is nakedly honest and so is very easily hurt by a careless word or response. The creation is part of the essence of the child who created it. It is the child's mind and heart given through expression and communication to those around him. In doing so the child has opened himself and is essentially defenseless.

HOW TO DEVELOP CREATIVE ABILITY

Conscious Work

In the last section we dealt with the issue of how easy it is to destroy creative ability. Fortunately it is also easy to encourage and develop creative ability. In this section we will deal with basic rules and concepts that will allow you, the parent or teacher, to develop your child's creative ability. Remember, every child is born with creative ability: Therefore it is not necessary to teach him, it is only necessary to guide him and encourage him in the development of his natural creative ability.

Earlier, in the discussion of the theory of the creative thought process, we identified its four parts:

1. Conscious Work
2. Subconscious Work
3. Inspiration
4. Theory

The teaching of the first part, conscious work, contains three essential ingredients:

1. The repetition of a creative exercise
2. Simplicity of Instruction
3. Complete removal of criticism

Understanding of these concepts and faithful adherence to them will produce terrific results. The removal or neglect of any one concept can be damaging or destructive to the process. Study the following directions carefully before beginning to work with your child.

1 - Repetition of a Creative Exercise

The primary creative exercise used in the CAD method is a technique called improvisation. The definition of the term improvise is "to compose, recite, play or sing on the spur of the moment: extemporize (on the piano)" (Mirriam-Webster). Long before music became written down, the primary means of musical expression was through improvisation. Up until the 20th Century, improvisation was an art expected of every musician. Most of the great musicians and composers prior to the 20th Century were famous in their day for their fantastic improvisations.

Improvisation as a tool for the development of creative ability works extremely well for several reasons. One, it is a demanding creative exercise for the conscious part of the process. Two, because it can be repeatedly practiced it can act as a trigger for the subconscious process. Three, during improvisation there can at times be enough relaxation of the conscious work process to allow communication from subconscious to conscious which thereby allows inspiration to occur. Four, instructions for improvisation can be very simple which serves to open the mind solely to the purpose of creative activity. In other words, the creative act can be completely separated from other types of brain activity so the focus on creativity can develop this ability exclusively.

In CAD level one, the use of a cassette/CD aides in the repetition aspect of the exercise. The cassette/CD provides a harmonic framework for the student to work with on a daily basis. The cassette/CD contains 28 separate exercises each to be used for a period of 1-2 weeks. By using this harmonic background correctly, i.e. practicing one exercise repeatedly for a period of 1-2 weeks, the student can continually practice solving the same creative problem. The cassette/CD aurally gives theoretical information to the student without any explanation being necessary. It also trains the students' ear to hear and understand the language of musical pitch and rhythm, thereby also developing his ability to 'speak' in a musical language. A multitude of styles and harmonies are provided in order to encourage and stimulate new ideas.

The crucial point of this section is the idea of repetition. Daily repetition or practice of the same exercise for a period of one to two weeks before continuing on to the next exercise is necessary for development. Without this repetition the student will not progress or develop his natural creative ability to a higher level.

2 - Simplicity of Instruction

In teaching an exercise to a child, simplicity of language and directions are very important. Too much complexity can confuse a child. Complexity can also disrupt the creative process by interfering with conscious focus on the creative aspects of an exercise. Ideally the student should be entirely focused on his creation of sound, without any thought of theory or intellectual understanding.

Rules are necessary however, so it is important to understand how to communicate them simply. One of the basic ingredients of every exercise is the key that it's in. A key is the group of notes which are available to be used; the key also excludes certain notes. A theoretical understanding of a given key could be very complicated, and is not necessary to the successful completion of an exercise. The understanding which is necessary is of a physical nature, i.e. where to put one's fingers. For example, to instruct a child how to play in the key of C major on a piano one simply needs to say play only on the white keys! To play in the key of F# pentatonic one needs to say play only on the black keys!

For a string player, the fingers are numbered and placed on tapes prepared in advance on the fingerboard (usually by the child's teacher). So for example, the instruction for the key of D pentatonic on the violin would be 'use fingers 1 and 3 on the A and E strings,' or in A major 'use 1, 2 and 3 on the A and E strings.'

These simplified instructions are provided for each exercise which means the parent need not have any theoretical knowledge at all. There are separate explanations given for the parents' general understanding of the material being presented. This information is provided solely for the instructor/parent and should not be given to the student unless a student specifically requests the information.

By keeping the instructions simple the parent/teacher will enable the child to focus completely on his musical creation. The child will not become frustrated or overburdened by unnecessary complications and will remain free to express himself artistically in a musical language.

3 - Complete Removal of Criticism

Rule #1 in CAD is "There's no such thing as a mistake!" This is true. It is also the first instruction or rule I introduce to a new CAD student. Criticism of any kind (this includes things like correct hand position or posture) is not allowed in CAD work. The reasons for this are numerous and extremely important.

1 - Criticism of the creation of a child takes away his ownership of the creation because the criticizer through his criticism recreates the music according to his own set of aesthetics. This interrupts the child's creative process and destroys the work already completed.
2 - Criticism of the creation suggests to the child that there is a right or wrong solution to a given creative problem. This is of course, not true.
3 - Criticism of the creation destroys the child's confidence in his ability to create.
4 - Criticism of the creation suggests to the child that he should try to 'second guess' the instructor's ideas in order to get the 'correct' answer to the creative exercise. This is impossible to do, and is detrimental to the child's own creative development. It also interrupts the child's search for his own best or honest solution to the exercise.
5 - Criticism of the student's posture, intonation, technique, tone, etc. distracts the student from focus on the creative act. There is plenty of opportunity to correct these other items during the regular practice. Remember, creativity is a separate specific ability which needs development. The brain cannot focus on more than one thing at a time.

By removing criticism, the freedom of choice is given to the student. Creative ability is the art of making choices. Through choices in sound (of beautiful or ugly, right or wrong, good or bad) the student develops his ability to make aesthetic judgments on a high level. Given this complete freedom of choice students will become confident in their search for the best within themselves. They do not need to be instructed to search for truth and beauty, they do it automatically. The reason for this stems from the human satisfaction of needs that go beyond the physical realm. Each student's search is unique, each student's creative solutions are unique. As Mozart says "But why my productions take from my hand that particular form and style that makes them Mozartish, and different from the works of other composers, is probably owing to the same cause which renders my nose so large or so aquiline, or, in short, makes it Mozart's, and different from those of other people. For I really do not study or aim at any originality."

Invariably the student will at some point ask the question "If there's no such thing as a mistake, why do I have to follow the rules of the exercise?" or "What happens if I play a note not in the key?" The correct response to this question is "You can't ever make a creative mistake. You can break the rules however and it's my job to explain them to you if that happens. CAD makes up the rules, you make up the music. As long as you follow the rules you cannot make a mistake. Your song belongs to you." I have never found a child who did not understand this concept.

It is now clear that criticism is destructive, however there are a few pitfalls to watch out for that are more subtle.

1 - Too Much Applause! It is easy to get excited with the music a child is creating and to respond positively. This is a good thing most of the time. However, if the instructor becomes very excited over one particular creation the student can become disturbed or distracted in the next assignments because he feels the need to repeat that particular performance or he fears being unable to produce another piece that is as good.

2 - 'Helpful' suggestions. Sometimes a student may start an exercise and may seem to have some difficulty getting ideas. This is perfectly normal. It is why repetition is necessary. The instructor may have some wonderful ideas and may wish to share them with the student. This urge must be resisted. You, the instructor, will not speed up the creative process for the student, you will merely slow it down or destroy it. Never give the student musical ideas or suggestions unless they are specified in the rules.

3 - Comparisons. Never compare one child's creation to another's. Each child moves at his own pace and has his own unique ideas. The early years are critical in the development both of ideas and confidence. Any criticism no matter how slight or in what form can be severely damaging.

Once, when teaching children CAD in a school in Paris, I noticed that the teachers were becoming very excited with certain students who were developing ideas very quickly. They applauded these children and complimented them. The other children, who were receiving no criticism but also very little attention, began to be less and less confident. In not applauding equally the teachers were making comparisons which detrimentally affected those students not receiving positive attention. We had a meeting and decided to try applauding all the children equally. Immediately the under-confident children began developing beautifully and gained much greater confidence by the end of the week.

It is important to understand that attention should always be positive in nature and should reward the creative search, (i.e. the work, not necessarily the end result). A simple "Good Work!" at the end of practice is sufficient. It is also nice and encouraging to compliment a work by mentioning that you liked it, or that it made you feel something special, but it is not necessary to do this all the time.

4 - Interruption of the creative process to correct a broken rule. Never interrupt an exercise to correct a broken rule. Wait until it is finished, compliment the student's work and then re-explain the rules so that he understands clearly. The reason for this is simply that the creative act is very concentrated and should never be interrupted.

Don't panic if you accidentally break one of these rules. Children are very strong and generally if you correct your mistakes they will quickly regain any confidence they might have lost.

Once again a quick review:

1 - Practice one exercise daily for 1-2 weeks following instructions carefully.
2 - Keep instructions as simple as possible. Keep the language of instruction as simple as possible.
3 - "There's No Such Thing As A Mistake!"
4 - Never Criticize
5 - Never interrupt the creative process or exercise to explain a broken rule.
6 - Never offer creative suggestions.
7 - Never compare children's creative abilities
8 - Never correct posture or technique during a CAD session.
9 - Don't single out one particular piece and over praise it.
10 - Do praise the creative work and occasionally compliment the expression.

Subconscious Work

As discussed earlier, subconscious work is triggered by conscious work. If conscious work is done correctly (without criticism) on a daily basis, the subconscious work will begin to occur both during practice and during rest or other activities. Repetition is the primary key to the subconscious process. This process will not be triggered without conscious repetitive hard work on a creative exercise.

Subconscious work cannot be observed except when it communicates to the conscious part of the brain. This communication, called inspiration, is at first subtle and hard to recognize. Later it becomes much more obvious and occurs with much greater rapidity.

Inspiration

One of the most remarkable incidents of inspiration that I have witnessed occurred several years ago. A six-year-old boy, who had studied Suzuki violin and CAD from the age of two, came in to his private lesson one day with a piece of notebook paper. On it he had drawn his own staff paper (paper with special lines used to write music on) and had written out a melody.

I asked his mother what it was, and she replied that she had been busy working and had given Jeffrey some paper to draw on. She thought he was just scribbling. I asked Jeffrey if he could play what he had written, and he said "Yes." He then played exactly what he had written down except he hadn't included a key signature. When I asked him what the name of the key was he replied "A Dorian" which was what he played. While he knew how to read music we hadn't discussed how to write it down or how to understand and write key signatures. (A key signature is a sign at the beginning of each line of music which indicates the key of a given piece). He did have a knowledge of the sounds and names of keys from CAD class and from practice with his CAD tape.

What is remarkable about this incident is that it is such a clear example of an inspiration occurring after repeated creative exercises. Jeffrey was also without an instrument, yet he was able to write down an entire melody which he heard in his inner ear. Obviously the inspiration was so strong and clear that this was not overly difficult for him.

This kind of inspiration occurs regularly during and between CAD practice as a result of the conscious creative work and subsequent subconscious work. Rarely do these inspirations get written down. How then, you may ask, does one identify them? The answer is by listening carefully to the student's improvisations. Each day as he repeats his assignment you will hear new ideas. One day you will hear a clearer, stronger melody (usually after one to two weeks of practice). This melody is probably inspired. Often after this inspiration, certain melodic fragments or even the entire piece, will recur in the next several days of improvisation. At this point the student is ready to move on. Often a student will recognize when he is ready to move on or when he is not ready. Students will sometimes say to me, "I think I need to work on this one some more" or "I'd like to practice this one longer."

Don't worry if you find you can't identify the inspiration. In the beginning it is often difficult. Students tend to play softly, searching for the best ideas and are not very sure of themselves. They often do not like their first ideas and don't really want to share them. If you are unsure simply do the exercise for two weeks and then move on. It is a good idea to review old exercises at a later date as new ideas or inspirations may occur as the student's creative ability develops.

Silent Ear Training

Throughout the exercises you will find suggestions to have the student practice something I call silent ear training. This serves several purposes, the most important of which is to stimulate the subconscious to communicate to the conscious in an inspired state. Other purposes include: One, bringing the student to a higher level of focus and concentration, two, helping the student to hear the harmony and structure of the exercise more clearly and therefore understand it aurally and three, to demonstrate how to use a conscious thought process in a creative way.

Silent Ear Training is basically the act of improvisation without an instrument. The student improvises in his mind melodic ideas while listening to the exercise. He does this without his instrument and without singing or humming. Therefore "silent" means 'mentally' not 'vocally' as in the "silent reading" of a book. After creating the melody 'silently' the student can then attempt to sing or play what he heard in his silent ear. (Bear in mind that this will not always be possible due to memory or instrumental limitations. The student should be made aware of this and be reassured that it is quite normal not to remember many of their ideas or to not be able to find the notes on their instrument right away.)

Sometimes the very concept of the silent ear is confusing to the student. A little game can help: Have the student close his eyes. Ask him to listen to the note you are going to play and to tell you, or raise a hand, when he can no longer hear it. Then, strike a note on the piano, holding it down and letting it fade very slowly. When the student says he can no longer hear it, ask him to listen more carefully because the note is still there.* Repeat the exercise. This time when he says he can't hear it anymore ask him to concentrate and try to hear it. Then try to sing it. Explain to him that even though the note is gone outside, it is there in his mind if he concentrates hard enough. This music which he can hear in his mind, which no one else can hear, is the music his mind creates and his 'silent ear' can hear.

I usually wait to introduce the silent ear until the student has improvised for a while, and then only after he has practiced the particular exercise for at least a week. The reason for this is simply that most students will not have a lot of ideas early in their creative work. They need to be exposed to enough music to provide a language for the silent ear. Also, practicing a particular exercise on the instrument first will heighten the subconscious response which will thereby provide ideas for the silent ear to work with. I have found that use of silent ear training greatly heightens a student's creative ability. After this exercise the music played by the student will very often be startlingly beautiful - more so than immediately preceding it.

After the student is able to use it the exercise of the silent ear can be used as often as he wishes: It need not be used only where suggested in the instructions.

* The note may actually be gone - but it is there in his silent ear.

Theory

Theory is introduced in two ways in CAD. One is through the rules of each exercise. The second way is through aural understanding of the music presented on the tape/CD. As a result of these two items in conjunction with the student's creative act a third way is introduced. Through his act of creation using the given rules and harmonic framework, the student begins to create his own musical theory. And though he doesn't articulate it or even necessarily understand it intellectually at first, his understanding is a deeper one because it is more innate, or natural.

Music is an aural art. The ear listens, develops, creates and eventually interprets what is created. Without this natural development the ear will be stunted and then so will creativity in a musical language.

To aid in the act of theoretical analysis I have included questions of a theoretical nature with each exercise. These are optional. If they are fun and/or interesting to the student they should be used. But if, on the other hand, the student finds them difficult or frustrating they should be saved until he is older or more advanced in his studies. Forcing a child to do something before he is ready will defeat the purpose not only at the moment but also in the future. In CAD, the most important aspects of study are in the art of creation itself - the actual daily improvisation.

The act of theoretical analysis and the act of creation are two separate processes of thought. Theoretical analysis is included in the theory of the creative process because it is at times necessary to use it to explain an inspiration. Theoretical understanding can also help begin the creative process on a higher level. It should be used as a trigger and not as the act of creation itself. If creation is done only theoretically it ceases to be inspired.

If too much theory is introduced too soon, it can hamper the freedom of choice which is so integral to the creative process. It is particularly damaging if the student comes to feel or sense that theory is the 'correct' way to solve a creative problem. The search for the best or most sincere solution to a given problem is the goal. Without that search, the subconscious can never be triggered to respond, and the creative problem would be solved only by the conscious part of the brain.

Remember, in the creative process theory always follows creation. Throughout history this is also true. Musicians and composers of the past may never have analyzed their music at all. It probably wasn't necessary.

DEALING WITH FEAR AND EGO

There are three types of fear certain children will need to overcome in order to successfully participate in the CAD program. Some children will have no fear, some will have one or another of these types to a greater or lesser degree. It is important therefore to understand these types of fear and the different solutions available to help children deal with them.

Type one is the 'fear of making mistakes.' Actually, in the case of CAD it is 'the fear of making mistakes and not being told.' Children with this fear tend to be children who are perfectionists. They work hard, study a lot and excel at most school activities. They have difficulty comprehending the idea that there could be a system of learning which stated as its main rule "there's no such thing as a mistake."

My first experience with a child of this type was in one of the first experimental CAD classes I ever taught. We played group games and then the children took turns playing solos while the other children listened. When it came to the solo turns I always asked for volunteers, and I always had to restrain the majority of the class because they all wanted a turn.

One day I noticed one little girl who never volunteered, though she had in the past. It seemed for a period of about a month she had not wanted a turn. Thinking she was just being polite offering her turn to the other children, I called on her and asked her to come up. At first she said "That's okay, someone else can have my turn." But when I insisted she said "I don't want a turn." She then burst into tears and ran from the room. I was amazed. What had happened?

I excused the class and sat down with this little girl. I asked her why she didn't want to play. She replied "I'm not very good at it. I don't make up good songs." I explained that that's why we practice doing it, to get better at it. Then she said, "But how can I get better at it if no one will tell me when I'm making mistakes? I know I'm making them because my music doesn't sound very good!" That's when I finally understood the problem and the fear. She didn't believe that there was no such thing as a mistake. Actually she believed that she was making mistakes and no one was telling her. She wanted to fix her mistakes but didn't know how. This girl was an excellent violinist. Her technique was exceptionally good because she worked very hard at it and was very respectful of her teacher's advice. She also cared deeply about all aspects of her training including CAD.

I quickly realized that simply restating "There's no such thing as a mistake" to this child would not be enough. She needed to understand why "there's no such thing as a mistake" in creative activity. I began by explaining that creativity is the act of making choices. If I made the choices for her she would never learn to make them herself, and would never develop her creative ability. The fact that she didn't like the music she created, didn't mean that it wasn't good. It simply meant that she had to try making new choices to satisfy her own sense of beauty or truth. What I as the teacher liked or disliked was irrelevant because it wasn't my creation.

I further went on to explain that in order to get better at this activity of making choices she had to practice. Just like she had to repeat hard parts in her pieces over and over to make them better, she had to practice CAD exercises to improve her ability to create music that she liked. Practice meant, in this instance, making choices and changing them if she didn't like them until she was satisfied. I explained that this practice would improve her creative ability.

After this conversation she was no longer crying and appeared much calmer. A week later she came to class with a rose and card thanking me for taking the time to explain things to her. From that day on she worked hard at her CAD exercises, never being afraid to take her turn. She soon became the first to volunteer when I asked. Years later when she was about to go on stage to give her first recital I asked her if she was nervous. She replied, "No, if I forget my pieces I'll just improvise!" She was 12 years old and she played a fantastic recital!

This fear of making mistakes (and not being told how to fix them) can be solved through conversation as clearly demonstrated above. Other fears such as the fear of the loss of conscious control are more complicated. These students want to quit before they have barely begun. They don't like the initial ideas they get when improvising and try to think up better ones with their conscious minds. At the beginning stages however this is practically impossible because they don't have a creative musical language to build upon yet. Therefore they draw a blank, they have no ideas. At this point they put down their instrument and refuse to play saying "I can't do it" or "I have no ideas" or most commonly "I don't know what to play." A couple of times I have even seen a student play a piece from his Suzuki repertoire like 'twinkle' or 'Minuet I' in order to avoid making up his own.

Conversation can be very helpful, but there are also certain games which can encourage these students. My first response to a student with this fear is to tell him, "play but don't think." I explain that he shouldn't worry about how the first notes sound. After he's played for a while then he can begin to judge what he does and doesn't like. "Don't think, just move your fingers and listen first. Your fingers will start to find notes you like if you let them, but it takes time and practice."

For some children the idea of playing without thinking is very scary. By saying "Don't Think" you can clarify that this is truly what you want from them. The next step is to give them an opportunity to "hide" while they try to play without thinking. In other words, give the child an opportunity to have some privacy while he judges himself. He needs to feel like he's the only judge, that no one else is listening critically.

This "hiding" can be accomplished in several ways. One, turn out the lights so that no one can see the child as he experiments. Many children love to play in the dark because they feel safer. Two, play with the child. They feel more comfortable for three reasons: They can play without your attention on them, they can play softer so that their music can't be heard by anyone but themselves, and they can witness the adult's struggle for ideas which is the same as their own. A third way of "hiding" is to turn the tape on very loud. The child can then play softer so that no one can listen but himself. A fourth way is to turn on the tape and leave the room to allow complete privacy for the child. These ways of hiding can also be combined; for example playing in the dark together, or turning the tape on loud and leaving the room.

An emphasis on rules can sometimes distract a nervous child from thoughts of creativity. For example, asking a child to play on one string while you play another and to switch whenever you do, turns the session into a technical game. Because he becomes involved in the technical game, he improvises freely without being aware of it. Soon he realized that the act of creation is not as difficult as he originally thought. He also realizes that he is pretty good at it and is less embarrassed to work at it.

Another idea is to play 'follow the leader.' Turn on the tape and ask the child to do whatever you do. Do simple things on open strings. Do silly things (like holding the bow upside down, or playing the violin like a guitar) to relax the child and make him laugh. Then switch roles. Ask the child to be leader. Children love to be in control and usually jump at the chance. Also, the child has greater confidence and pride in his ideas if someone else tries to mimic them.

The hardest part of CAD for children is usually the first attempt to improvise. It's similar to the first lesson in learning to ride a bicycle. It's exciting but also a little scary. A parent would usually hold on to the back of the bike for quite a while to balance it and to instill confidence in the child. At a certain point when it appears the child is ready the parent lets go and the child keeps going, often unaware that the parent is no longer holding on. In CAD this is just like the parent playing with the child or playing follow the leader, to establish the child's first sense of understanding and confidence. Once established the parent lets go and the child can continue forever on his own, just like on the bike!

Ultimately, doing is developing. Talking about how to ride a bike won't teach a child to ride, similarly talking about how to develop creativity won't develop creativity: Practicing will. But sometimes, as mentioned earlier, talking is a means to achieve doing. There are several approaches to talking about creativity, some better suited to younger children and some better suited to older children. Here is a list of possible topics:

1. Why there's no such thing as a mistake
2. A matter of individual choice
3. The search for truth and beauty
4. How Mozart worked
5. Practice and repetition apply to creative ability too
6. The creative process
7. A creative twinkler

1. Why there's no such thing as a mistake

There's no such thing as a mistake because when you make up a song, you as the creator own it. It belongs to you, just as your thoughts belong to you. No one can tell you what to create, because if they did they would be the creator. My saying that something you create is a mistake is just another way of saying that I would create it differently. Well of course I would - I'm a different person. That doesn't make my way right and your way wrong. Every person in the world creates differently, just like every person has a different shaped nose. No two people look exactly alike, no two people think exactly alike, and no two people create exactly alike.

2. A matter of individual choice

Creating music is the art of making choices. The creator must constantly choose between the available notes to create a piece. The choice is not a matter of right or wrong, rather it is one of like or dislike. The person creating is the only person who can make those choices. No two people like or dislike exactly the same things. Just like some people prefer vanilla ice cream and some like chocolate - some prefer maple walnut! In order to find what you like you might have to try some you don't like. How would you ever know you prefer vanilla to chocolate if you never tried both. Choosing notes is the exact same thing. You have to try many different ones before you find the ones you like (and you will have to play some you don't like along the way).

All great creative geniuses ultimately search for one of two things: Truth or beauty. Sometimes they search for both. Indeed there is always beauty in the artistic expression of truth. These are the highest goals. They are difficult to attain. Great discipline, repetition, concentration, and personal sincerity of expression are required.

Above all it is important to realize that the creative process is a search. A search which takes a long time, perhaps even a lifetime. Artistic searching never really ends because it is a process by which we can learn and continue to grow. Pieces which we compose along the way are more like pictures taken on a long journey. They reflect our growth and development up to that point in time.

4. How Mozart worked

Mozart, contrary to the myths which surround his name, worked very hard to develop his creative ability. As a young boy, Mozart studied composition exercises given to him by his father. Later he practiced counterpoint on a daily basis. (Counterpoint is a creative exercise with very complicated rules.) In his concerts, Mozart regularly improvised cadenzas and often improvised melodic lines and decorations. He was also a famous improviser of whole pieces in his day. When he wasn't performing, improvising or practicing counterpoint he would most likely be composing new pieces from ideas he worked on in his mind.

His regular conscious creative work triggered constant subconscious creative work which rewarded Mozart with whole inspired compositions. Mozart had a very fine memory and was able to write down his inspirations in public places thus causing much of the myth which surrounds his name.

5. Practice and repetition apply to creative ability too!

Most students understand that to achieve greatness in performance, practice is required. The better and longer the practice, the quicker the development of performance ability. To master a technically difficult passage, repetition is necessary. In fact, without repetition, development is practically impossible.

Creative Ability Development works that same way. With practice and repetition any student can develop their natural creative ability to a high level. The longer the practice, the greater the number of repetitions, the quicker and greater the development of creative ability.

The primary difference between the two is that creative exercises develop the thought processes of the brain, while performance exercises develop the accuracy and physical ability of the fingers, hands and arms. In all other respects the concept of practice and repetition works the same in performance and creative ability.

6. The creative process

For an older child, an understanding of the theory of the creative process can encourage participation in what he may perceive as an impossible task. Older children are very self-critical but can be persuaded to work at a difficult task if they can be made to understand the scientific underpinnings of what they are attempting to accomplish.

A quick explanation (of how conscious creative exercises trigger subconscious creative work, and how through subconscious work, inspiration is achieved) may intrigue and encourage a hesitant, under-confident student. Particularly if the student is used to controlling his own achievement through his own practice or study.

In a sense, through this explanation you are giving the student greater control of the teaching aspects of CAD. With this feeling of greater control the student can become more confident of his ability to develop creatively.

7. A creative twinkler

It is important for students to understand that no matter what their age, when they start CAD they are essentially "creative twinklers." A creative twinkler is another way of saying that the student is a beginner in his creative studies. Just as at one time the student was a beginner on his instrument and had to learn twinkle (a common first piece), he is now a beginner at creative development.

Because, though a certain amount of innate creative ability exists in all children, if it has not been developed their ability is probably at the level of a 5-year-old. Therefore, the student should not be discouraged if he is older but feels inadequate in his creative ideas. He needs to understand that creativity does not develop without practice. With practice his ability will develop rapidly, ideas will come more easily and with greater abundance. As he continues to practice the ideas will become more defined and pleasurable and he will be able to bring the level of his creative ability up to the level of his performance ability.

Acknowledgment of being a 'creative twinkler' can help older students accept their early difficulties. They can then feel less pressured to immediately succeed while at the same time be encouraged to see how well they can develop with practice. A 5-year-old and a 15-year-old may sound the same in terms of their musical ideas when first starting out. This does not in any way suggest that either of them lack the ability to develop their creativity to a very high level.

In this chapter, we have dealt with two kinds of fear: The fear of making creative 'mistakes,' and fear of loss of conscious control. These fears related primarily to the creative act itself. But there exists another fear familiar to many students which is only superficially related to creative exercises. This is the fear of performing. It is particularly important to address this fear if the student is studying CAD with his peers or siblings present.

Anytime a student plays and another person hears him it is a CAD performance. Because the creative act is much more personally revealing than the basic act of performing it is crucially important that the student be respected and applauded. He should never be criticized or ignored by his peers or siblings if they are present.

In my CAD group classes there are two rules I use to deal with this fear: #1 is 'Applause and Silence.' The 'Applause and Silence' rule means that if a student is playing, the others present are silent; when the student finishes the others present applaud him. The #2 rule is 'never criticize a friend.' This is simply an extension of the first rule of CAD "There's no such thing as a mistake."

If these two rules are followed during CAD practice the student will develop confidence in his creative ability as well as in his ability to perform. This confidence can even carry over to his regular performances in recitals, etc. If these rules are not followed the results can be very damaging to the student's self-esteem and thereby to his creative ability development.

It is important to always remember that creative expression comes from the deepest emotional and intellectual part of a human being. Creative expression belongs to each person and is uniquely his. Criticizing that expression is far worse than criticizing one's nose or speech or hair. Therefore it takes great courage to be expressive and even greater courage to be creative.

Never criticize a child for being fearful, or for playing softly, or for making ugly sounds. What he is expressing is real emotion which can eventually become great aesthetic expression.

Once I had a student who for the entire first year of CAD classes would only make scratching noises on her violin. At home her mother said, she played beautiful melodies with the CAD tape. During her second year she began to play very softly in class and as the year went by played stronger and stronger. She was hiding that first year, afraid to share her ideas and expressions with the class, while at home she was unafraid. Or perhaps there was another reason for those early scratches. Whatever it was, it was not important. What was important was that she continued to come to class and participate and eventually began to express herself in a way which was aesthetically beautiful. She learned to trust her classmates and feel safe in the atmosphere of the class. She also learned that, no matter what she did, I would never criticize her expression.

Another little boy came to class his first year and refused to play. He loved to be there and to play games which didn't require him to use his instrument, but would not play any other games or solos. Thinking of this little girl from the other class, I asked him one day to make the ugliest sound he could on his cello. He thought this was funny and quickly complied producing the exact same scratching sounds the little girl had made. This I realized, was a safe sound. He then participated in the next game which required him to play his cello, happily making 'ugly' sounds. Eventually I asked him to play a beautiful sound and he did. He was still afraid of this and quickly reverted to the ugly sound. I feel it is safe to assume that this child will continue to progress to the point of trusting his classmates and teacher to respect his ideas and will eventually share them with the class. He is, at home, playing with the tape. He is still in his first year.

These two are extreme cases of some of the kinds of fear and some interesting solutions to the problems discussed in this chapter. I'm sure there are many more solutions I have yet to discover but in nine years I have never seen one student give up because of fear. Hopefully, I never will.

GETTING STARTED

The very first CAD lesson or practice is invariably the hardest to teach. The introduction of concepts never before studied, the facing of an instrument without specific instructions of how to use it, and the overwhelming number of choices of pitch and rhythm that the student is faced with may make him uneasy, uncomfortable and unhappy. He may want to walk away before he begins. Therefore we must approach this first lesson with great care, preparation and understanding.

The most important aspect of this first lesson is the introduction and confirmation of the number one rule "There's No Such Thing As A Mistake." Explain that since the student is making up the song no one can criticize it. If anyone criticizes it he becomes the creator of the song. Therefore you, the adult instructor, will never criticize his musical creation.

Children love to test this rule, perhaps because they don't really believe it's true. They begin to do all kinds of silly things: For example, they might play behind the bridge, hold the violin like a guitar, hold the bow upside down, bow over the fingerboard - in essence do all the things they've been told not to do on their instrument. With the exception of something that might damage the instrument, you must allow the silliness. There are two reasons why you should. First, if you criticize them they won't believe the number one rule is true. This is deadly. Second, after the initial testing phase the ideas of color contrasts and interesting uses of their instruments becomes part of the creative process. Incidentally, this testing phase may not occur immediately, in some cases it may not occur at all.

EXPLAINING THE RULES

After you have explained the number one rule (there's no such thing as a mistake) it is time to begin to work with the tape/CD. It is good to compare the rules of each exercise to the rules of a game. Each exercise is like it's own separate game with its own set of rules. In order to play the game, the rules need to be understood. It is important to stress that the rules are not the point of the exercise, just the means to be able to begin the exercise. Tell the student you will never interrupt the game to work on the rules. They will be introduced in the beginning and repeated at the end if necessary. Remember to keep your language as simple as possible when explaining rules and only give students the information they need, don't elaborate.

FINDING THE FIRST NOTES

Sometimes the hardest part for the student is finding the first notes. It's kind of like jumping into a pool when you don't know how to swim. A very frightening prospect. To help the student overcome this fear I sometimes give the student his first note. For most children that's all that is necessary. Once they begin they usually think the game is easy and they start to enjoy it. Particularly when they play the exercise without receiving criticism and they are also praised at the end for their work.

But sometimes the student plays the given note and stops, complaining that he doesn't know what to do next. At this point ask him if he liked the note. If he liked it he should play it again, if not he should try a different one. By limiting the notes in the initial exercise to the two open strings the choices are extremely limited. This makes the choosing easier. Once he begins let him continue uninterrupted.

After the exercise or in the case of a student who absolutely refuses to begin it is wise to discuss the nature of creativity in the following way. The game or exercise is about making choices. The choices are not right or wrong but rather, like or dislike. No one can tell someone else what to like. Some people like chocolate ice cream, some people like vanilla, some people like strawberry. Musical creation is the same way. Some people like some notes, other people like other notes. The choice is up to each individual person. By learning which notes he likes or dislikes, he is developing his ability to make choices and making these choices allows him to make up his own music. That's why "there's no such thing as a mistake" - there are no right or wrong answers, only what each person likes or dislikes.

This conversation or explanation should relieve any doubts or fears the child still has. It is important to help the child get started as quickly and easily as possible. For further ideas on this subject see the chapter "Dealing with Fear and Ego."

Often none of these problems arise and the beginning is simple and easy. Usually, once the student plays an exercise he is on his way to a continuing pattern of growth and development of his creative ability. The ease or difficulty with which he begins is irrelevant to the eventual development of his creative ability and in no way indicates or determines any lack of natural creative ability.

CAD - TIME OF DEVELOPMENT

I have found after years of teaching CAD that there seems to be a pattern of growth associated with creative ability. It seems that a certain period of time is necessary for student to achieve new levels of ability. These levels of ability are characterized by certain outward signs.

Level I - level one begins from day one and lasts 1-3 years. It is usually characterized by a quiet style of playing. The student is beginning his search for what he likes and is more introspective. He may at times be experimental, aggressive or timid for no apparent reason. These are all normal expressions of the search for communicative and beautiful or honest creations.

During this first level there is often a jump at about the six month point to a more developed sense and awareness of the tape and how the student fits in with it. There is a greater overall cohesiveness and a slightly more outgoing tone.

Level II - Sometime during the period between the second and fourth year there is a major leap into a much greater creative sense which is almost always accompanied by a much greater tone and outward expression. This leap seems at times to take place overnight. Often at this time there is a great improvement in the student's overall playing. His tone, vibrato, expression and confidence improve dramatically as does his general fluency and flexibility. His musical ideas are more mature and beautiful and come easily to him.

Level III - Level 3 occurs sometime in the sixth or seventh year. It is characterized by a hunger for greater technical challenges. Students will often begin exploring new forms and keys as well as harmonies. They may also express a desire to compose music at this time. Their musical ideas at this level are quite mature and beautiful and are often very expressive. They are able to play independently (without accompaniment) and create form, development and harmony as well as melody.

Of course not every child will follow this pattern of development. Some will move quicker and some will move slower. As with all musical artistic studies, practice is essential. More practice results in greater and faster development of any child.

It is very important to remember that creative ability takes time to develop just as any ability takes time to develop. It takes years of practice!

Young children are both extremely fragile and extremely capable. They have a vast ability to learn and develop while at the same time they are extremely sensitive to adult approval or criticism. The power of positive encouragement from parents and teachers is very great. The destructive power of criticism may be even greater.

Children need tools with which to develop. They also need to practice with those tools. Without the use of tools and without the discipline of repetition a child cannot develop his ability to its greatest potential.

It is important to recognize as an adult the difference between technique and expression. Failure to recognize this difference may result in improper guidance or criticism from the adult who does not understand the unique perspective of the child. The mastery of technique may require many years beyond childhood while the mastery of expression begins much earlier. Development of muscle coordination is also a factor in early childhood technical expression.

Talent is not inborn!

Simplicity of instruction or guidance is necessary. A child learns through doing, not through explanations or complicated instructions. Theory follows creation. Understanding follows experience. Complicated instructions will only slow down the process.

The role of the adult is to be the audience, the encouragement, the catalyzer. Never should the adult be the creator.

If taught properly, creative development of a young child can promote self-esteem, artistic ability, confidence in self-expression, and joy in the sharing of creative ability. A proper group environment, one lacking in criticism, can stimulate these characteristics to a very high level.

PART III

EXERCISES

EXPLANATION OF INSTRUCTIONS

There are six parts to each exercise: Part one is a diagram of the finger pattern to be used and a written explanation of how to describe the key simply to the student. "Clicks" refers to the number of clicks that can be heard before the exercise begins. The purpose of the clicks is to let the student know the tempo (or speed) of the piece before he begins, as well as to let him know when to begin. The number of clicks varies depending on the speed and/or the meter (beats per measure) of the exercise. The following is an explanation of the diagram:

Key of A Major
Explanations of Diagram for Violin

Horizontal lines refer to tapes often placed on a beginner's violin in first position. Fingers may be placed on the tapes as shown here on the A and E strings, or above or below the tapes as shown here on the D and G strings.

Darkened circles are for advanced students only. Stars (★) denote the tonic of the key and in some cases may be used to start and/or end the piece. (The stars are used as an exercise only and do not indicate a right or wrong way to end a piece: Many solutions are possible.)

Use the body of the violin to determine the correct use of strings if you are unsure.

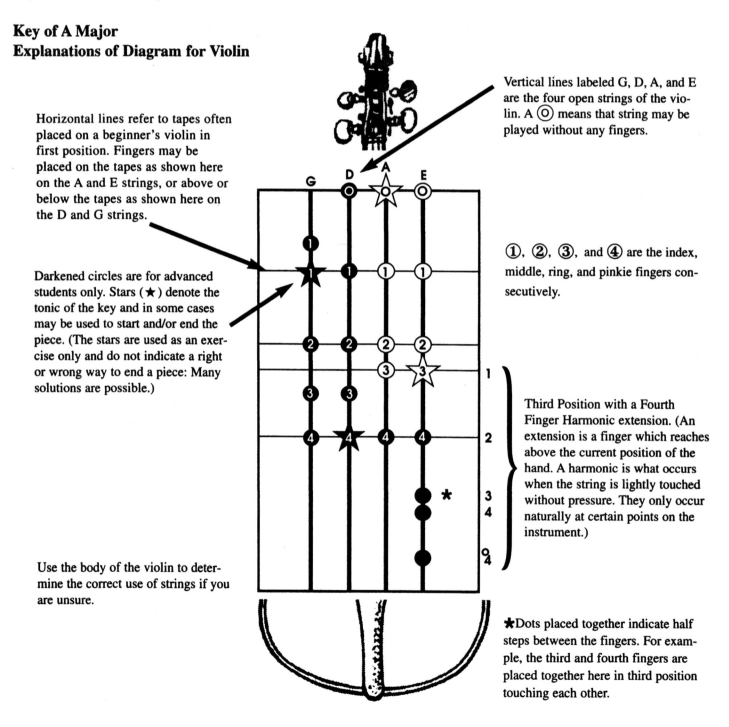

Vertical lines labeled G, D, A, and E are the four open strings of the violin. A Ⓞ means that string may be played without any fingers.

①, ②, ③, and ④ are the index, middle, ring, and pinkie fingers consecutively.

Third Position with a Fourth Finger Harmonic extension. (An extension is a finger which reaches above the current position of the hand. A harmonic is what occurs when the string is lightly touched without pressure. They only occur naturally at certain points on the instrument.)

★Dots placed together indicate half steps between the fingers. For example, the third and fourth fingers are placed together here in third position touching each other.

Please be sure to use the correct level of difficulty for the student. In the beginning even an advanced student should use the basic finger pattern. As the student becomes more advanced both creatively and technically the advanced finger patterns and ranges can and should be added.

Part two is called 'Basic Instructions.' All students should do these first before attempting the more difficult exercises in the advanced instructions (part three). It is important to work freely with the music to develop the creative process, particularly the subconscious response to the act of improvisation. Later, when the process is working easily, the more advanced instructions can heighten the subconscious response, but only if the free improvisation has been done first.

The advanced instructions of part three should be used only after the student has improvised with the exercise for at least a week using the basic instructions. Then, each exercise of the advanced instructions should be done, one per week. This can be done as a review exercise as the student moves on to a new piece. With a younger or beginning student, these instructions could be saved until the student has completed the entire tape using only basic instructions. Use the advanced instructions at your own discretion.

Part four, About the Music, is aimed at the parent or teacher. It provides theoretical information about the exercise. It is there so that if the student has questions regarding the piece, the parent or teacher has information with which to guide the student's understanding.

A better way of guiding the student's understanding is provided in parts five and six. Part five provides 'listening questions': questions which the student may try to answer by listening to the music. Part six provides the answers to those questions. These sections should be used like a game - for fun. They are a means to explore the music, listen to it more carefully, and understand it in a more theoretical manner. Some questions may seem simple while others are very difficult: Use your discretion in introducing them to the student. Also be sure you understand the answer before you ask the question. The parent or teacher may want to refer to part four before trying part five with a student.

1/19/2020 -ex. 1

Exercise #1

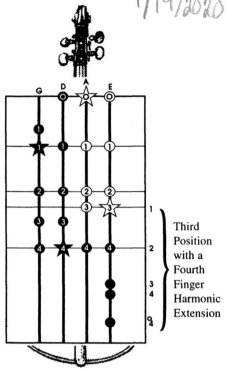

Third Position with a Fourth Finger Harmonic Extension

① **Key: A major** (student may use open A and E strings, and fingers 1, 2, and 3 on A and E. The second finger should be placed touching the third finger as it is in the Twinkle Variations of Suzuki Book One.)

Advanced Finger Pattern: Use all strings as described in the diagram. Note that open G string cannot be used, but can be replaced by a first finger, lowered into half position. Also notice that the third finger is raised on D and G strings. Third position may also be used on the E string with a fourth finger extending beyond into fourth position. This extended fourth finger should be played as a harmonic: The finger lightly touches the string but does not press it down to the fingerboard.

Clicks: 4

② **Basic Instructions:**
Using the finger pattern for A major (above) the student may play anything he wants. He cannot make a mistake since it is his own creation. The instructor should never interrupt the student once the playing has begun, (even if the student is using the wrong key or finger pattern). Upon completion, compliment the student and repeat the exercise three to four times. If there is a confusion regarding the finger pattern, explain it again between repetitions.

③ **Advanced Instructions:**
Exercise #1 - Sing the words "what's the answer to my question?" with the solo violin and then the cello at the beginning of the exercise.

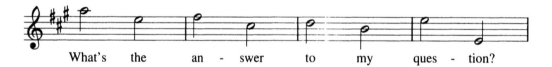

What's   the   an - swer   to   my   ques - tion?

Listen to this melody in the cello as you improvise over it.

Exercise #2 - Change your rhythm, articulation or dynamic with each new "what's the answer to my question?"

Exercise #3 - Listen carefully to the melody played by the violin. Try to play on the opposite string of the solo in the recording. You will have to change often.

Exercise #4 - Listen to the rhythms (the speed of the notes) of the solo violin part and try to match them. Do not match the notes themselves. Notice that the rhythm changes with each "what's the answer to my question?"

Exercise #5 - Notice the holes or spaces in the solo violin part and try to fill them in with quicker notes.

Exercise #6 - Attempt to overlap rhythmic patterns by imitating the previous rhythm of the solo violin as it changes to a new one every "what's the answer to my question?" phrase.

Solo Violin:

Improviser:

④ **About the Music:**

"What's the answer to my question?" is in the form of a passacaglia, though in this case in a duple meter as opposed to the more traditional baroque passacaglia which was written in a triple meter. A passacaglia is basically a set of variations over a repeated bass line. In this case the bass line is presented first in the solo violin, then taken over by the cello until the end where it is then presented in a chorale style. The melodic variations presented by the violin are arranged in a progressively faster rhythmic development and are then presented in a reversed order leaving out the eighth and ninth variation and adding a new one at the end.

Sometimes a child will ask, "what is the question, or what is the answer?" referring to the title. "What's the answer to my question?" is a philosophical title: The 'question' is the ostinato bass line or harmonic underpinning of the exercise, the 'answer' is the student's improvised response to the question. So of course there are many possible answers but only one question.

⑤ **Listening Questions:**

#1 - How many times can you find the melody "What's the answer to my question?" (See Advanced instructions Exercise #1) "Who played it?"

#2 - The violin plays 9 different melodies over "What's the answer to my question?" then repeats them backwards. Which ones get left out the second time? Were any new ones added?

⑥ **Answers:**

though a piece of it is at the very beginning of the song.

#2 - The eighth and ninth variation get left out the second time. There is one new one at the end

The first and last were played by the violin, the rest were played by the cello.

#1 - 2!

Exercise #2

① **Key: A major** (student may use open A and E strings, and fingers 1, 2, and 3 on A and E. The second finger should be placed touching the third finger as it is in the Twinkle Variations of Suzuki Book One.)

Advanced Finger Pattern: Use all strings as described in the diagram. Note that open G string cannot be used, but can be replaced by a first finger, lowere into half position. Also notice that the third finger is raised on D and G strings Third position may also be used on the E string with a fourth finger extending beyond into fourth position. This extended fourth finger should be played as a harmonic: The finger lightly touches the string but does not press it down to the fingerboard.

Clicks: 6

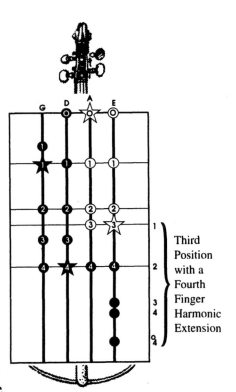

② **Basic Instructions:**

Using the finger pattern for A major (above) the student may play anything he wants. He cannot make a mistake since it is his own creation. The instructor should never interrupt the student once the playing has begun, (even if the student is using the wrong key or finger pattern). Upon completion, compliment the student and repeat the exercise three to four times. If there is a confusion regarding the finger pattern, explain it again between repetitions.

③ **Advanced Instructions:**

Exercise #1 - Listen for the "What's the answer to my question?" melody. You will find it in the cello part in this exercise, doubled by the piano. Listen to it as you improvise over it.

Exercise #2 - Listen to the "What's the answer to my question?" melody and change your rhythm, dynamic or articulation each time there is a repeat of the cello melody. How many different ways can you find to play your violin? Some suggestions: Pizzicato, violin upside down, bow on the bridge, bow on the fingerboard, bow upside down, bow bouncing etc.

Exercise #3 - Listen to the violins and try not to play the same notes. Try to play on a different string whenever possible.

Exercise #4 - Try to play in the spaces left by the longer held notes in the violins. Notice how the second violin often fills in the spaces left by the first violin in the first half of the piece. In the second half the second violin drops out leaving more room for the improviser to fill in the spaces.

④ **About the Music:**

Like the first exercise, this one is also a passacaglia using the same bass line, only this time it's in the more traditional triple meter. The violin parts are written as a loose canon, meaning that the first violin plays a melody which is then played by the second violin while the first violin continues with a new part. Both violins play the same part but one starts 8 bars before the other. (Common examples of canons are the folk songs "Row, Row, Row Your Boat" or "Frere Jacques.") In the exercise, the canon is played once with two violins and is then heard only by the solo violin.

⑤ **Listening Questions:**

#1 - How many times did you hear "What's the answer to my question?" played by both the cello and piano?

#2 - Are all the phrases canonic? If not, which are not?

⑥ **Answers:**

#1 - 21

#2 - No - The first and last phrases are not canonic in the first half of the piece (or the first and ninth phrase of the first violin)

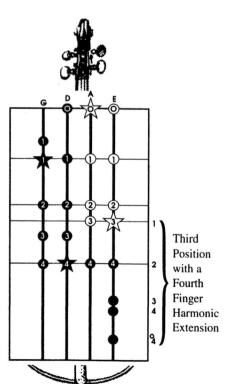

Third
Position
with a
Fourth
Finger
Harmonic
Extension

Exercise #3

CD Track
4

① **Key: A major** (student may use open A and E strings, and fingers 1, 2, and 3 on A and E. The second finger should be placed touching the third finger as it is in the Twinkle Variations of Suzuki Book One.)

Advanced Finger Pattern: Use all strings as described in the diagram. Note that open G string cannot be used, but can be replaced by a first finger, lowered into half position. Also notice that the third finger is raised on D and G strings. Third position may also be used on the E string with a fourth finger extending beyond into fourth position. This extended fourth finger should be played as a harmonic: The finger lightly touches the string but does not press it down to the fingerboard.

Clicks: 4

② **Basic Instructions:**

Using the finger pattern for A major (above) the student may play anything he wants. He cannot make a mistake since it is his own creation. The instructor should never interrupt the student once the playing has begun, (even if the student is using the wrong key or finger pattern). Upon completion, compliment the student and repeat the exercise three to four times. If there is a confusion regarding the finger pattern, explain it again between repetitions.

③ **Advanced Instructions:**

Exercise #1: listen to the piece carefully. You will hear three sections; one with melody, followed by one without, and ending with the one with melody. Play carefully avoiding the melody in the first and third sections, but play freely in the second section.

Exercise #2: Silently sing a melody in your head while listening to the piece. Try then to sing it out loud and then finally, to play it on your instrument. You probably won't play or sing exactly what you imagine in your silent singing. This is just a way of creating some new ideas, by thinking and improvising in your mind without your instrument.

④ **About the Music:**

This piece is a simple song form with three sections. The first and third sections are exactly the same, and the middle section differs only because the melody is left out and the harmony is filled in. This creates an ABA form.

⑤ **Listening Questions:**

#1 - There are three sections in this piece: Which two are exactly the same?

⑥ **Answers:**

#1 - The first and the third.

Exercise #4

① **Key: A major** (student may use open A and E strings, and fingers 1, 2, and 3 on A and E. The second finger should be placed touching the third finger as it is in the Twinkle Variations of Suzuki Book One.)

Advanced Finger Pattern: Use all strings described in the diagram. Note that open G string cannot be used, but can be replaced by a first finger, lowered into half position. Also notice that the third finger is raised on D and G strings. Third position may also be used on the E string with a fourth finger extending beyond into fourth position. This extended fourth finger should be played as a harmonic: The finger lightly touches the string but does not press it down to the fingerboard.

Clicks: 4

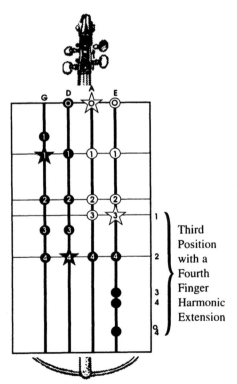

Third Position with a Fourth Finger Harmonic Extension

② **Basic Instructions:**

Using the finger pattern for A major (above) the student may play anything he wants. He cannot make a mistake since it is his own creation. The instructor should never interrupt the student once the playing has begun, (even if the student is using the wrong key or finger pattern). Upon completion, compliment the student and repeat the exercise three to four times. If there is a confusion regarding the finger pattern, explain it again between repetitions.

③ **Advanced Instructions:**

Exercise #1: Match the rhythms of the melody without playing the same notes. Maintain these rhythms in the middle section which has no melody.

Exercise #2: Improvise staying always on the opposite string of the melody in the first and third sections. Though there is no violin playing this melody, you will be able to tell which string to play on by listening carefully.

Exercise #3: Create a rhythm much slower than the one in the melody and maintain it while improvising. It may help to imagine, sing, and/or clap the idea first.

Exercise #4: By now you have heard this exercise a number of times and realize that the first and third sections contain a melody while the second section does not. The harmonic pattern of the first and second sections are exactly the same. Try to improvise an accompanying figure to the first and third sections. For example: a rhythm that matches the left hand of the piano (the lower part), or a part played pizzicato. In the second section create your own melodic part.

④ **About the Music:**

This piece is similar to the song form of exercise #3. It also has three sections with the middle section deleting the melody. It has a few differences however, one being the much quicker tempo. The other difference is in the form of the piece. Each of the sections has two distinct parts, an A and a B. They are played as follows: AAB aab AB- (the third time the A occurs only once).

⑤ **Listening Questions:**

#1 - One section of this piece has no melody. Which section is it?

⑥ **Answers:**

#1 - The middle section.

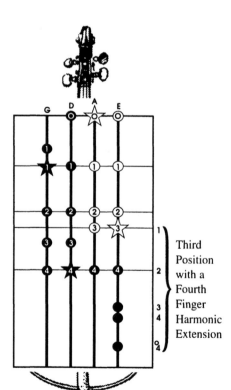

Third
Position
with a
Fourth
Finger
Harmonic
Extension

Exercise #5

① **Key: A major** (student may use open A and E strings, and fingers 1, 2, and 3 on A and E. The second finger should be placed touching the third finger as it is in the Twinkle Variations of Suzuki Book One.)

Advanced Finger Pattern: Use all strings described in the diagram. Note that open G string cannot be used, but can be replaced by a first finger, lowered into half position. Also notice that the third finger is raised on D and G strings. Third position may also be used on the E string with a fourth finger extending beyond into fourth position. This extended fourth finger should be played as a harmonic: The finger lightly touches the string but does not press it down to the fingerboard.

Clicks: 3

② **Basic Instructions:**

Using the finger pattern for A major (above) the student may play anything he wants. He cannot make a mistake since it is his own creation. The instructor should never interrupt the student once the playing has begun, (even if the student is using the wrong key or finger pattern). Upon completion, compliment the student and repeat the exercise three to four times. If there is a confusion regarding the finger pattern, explain it again between repetitions.

③ Advanced Instructions:

Exercise #1: Listen to the cello part and hear how it repeats. You can sing the words "what's the answer to my question?" to this cello line even though the notes are different from the original version. Change your articulation every time the cello line repeats.

Exercise #2: Match the rhythmic pulse of the piano with your own rhythms. Notice that it changes with every repeat of the cello line.

Exercise #3: Change your rhythms when the piano changes but do not imitate the piano rhythm itself. Instead, create your own.

④ About the Music:
This piece is again a passacaglia like the first two exercises. This one is in a triple meter with a set of rhythmic variations played over it by the piano. Each phrase develops to a greater rhythmic excitement until the end. The string quartet provides a harmonic progression which does not change throughout the piece.

⑤ How many rhythmic variations are there? Hint: the variations equal the number of times the cello line repeats.

⑥ Answer:

uǝ⊥

Exercise #6

CD Track 7

① Key: A major (student may use open A and E strings, and fingers 1, 2, and 3 on A and E. The second finger should be placed touching the third finger as it is in the Twinkle Variations of Suzuki Book One.)

Advanced Finger Pattern: Use all strings described in the diagram. Note that open G string cannot be used, but can be replaced by a first finger, lowered into half position. Also notice that the third finger is raised on D and G strings. Third position may also be used on the E string with a fourth finger extending beyond into fourth position. This extended fourth finger should be played as a harmonic: The finger lightly touches the string but does not press it down to the fingerboard.

Clicks: 6

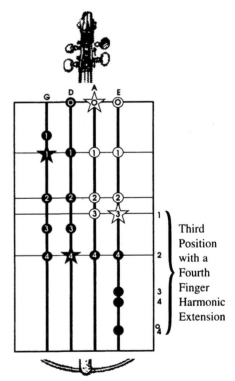

Third Position with a Fourth Finger Harmonic Extension

② Basic Instructions:
Using the finger pattern for A major (above) the student may play anything he wants. He cannot make a mistake since it is his own creation. The instructor should never interrupt the student once the playing has begun, (even if the student is using the wrong key or finger pattern). Upon completion, compliment the student and repeat the exercise three to four times. If there is a confusion regarding the finger pattern, explain it again between repetitions.

③ Advanced Instructions:

Exercise #1: Imagine a melody in your head while listening to the music. Try to remember some of it and play it on your instrument.

Exercise #2: Pick a rhythm and try to maintain it while improvising. For example a simple repeated ♩. (dotted half note) which equals one note per bar or perhaps a more complicated ♩ ♪♩ rhythm.

④ About the Music:

This little piece is a waltz, which is a dance in moderate to fast triple meter. It is recorded using both synthesized and real instruments.

⑤ Listening Questions:

All the instruments in this recording are synthesized except for one. Can you tell which instrument is not synthesized?

⑥ Answers:

The Piano

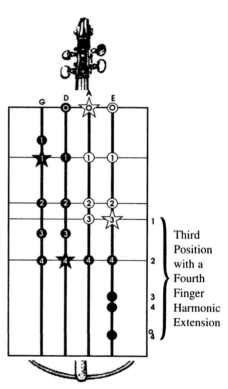

Exercise #7

① Key: A major (student may use open A and E strings, and fingers 1, 2, and 3 on A and E. The second finger should be placed touching the third finger as it is in the Twinkle Variations of Suzuki Book One.)

Advanced Finger Pattern: Use all strings described in the diagram. Note that open G string cannot be used, but can be replaced by a first finger, lowered into half position. Also notice that the third finger is raised on D and G strings. Third position may also be used on the E string with a fourth finger extending beyond into fourth position. This extended fourth finger should be played as a harmonic: The finger lightly touches the string but does not press it down to the fingerboard.

Third Position with a Fourth Finger Harmonic Extension

Clicks: 4

② Basic Instructions:

Using the finger pattern for A major (above) the student may play anything he wants. He cannot make a mistake since it is his own creation. The instructor should never interrupt the student once the playing has begun, (even if the student is using the wrong key or finger pattern). Upon completion, compliment the student and repeat the exercise three to four times. If there is a confusion regarding the finger pattern, explain it again between repetitions.

③ Advanced Instructions:

Exercise #1: Listen to the whole piece. You will hear that the first and last sections are the same but the middle is different. The first and last sections leave spaces between the melodies for a response from the improviser. Try to fill these spaces with a similar melody but a different rhythm. In the middle section play a continuous melody.

Exercise #2: Follow the instructions in exercise #1 above with the following change: Fill the spaces in the first and third sections with the same rhythms but different notes. It may help to sing or imagine your musical ideas first.

④ **About the Music:**
This exercise is in an ABA form with the A section being a question/answer form in 6/8. 6/8 is a triple division of two beats per bar. The middle section (B) is not a question/answer form and is in 2/4 which is a duple division of two beats per bar.

For example:
A section

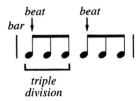

B Section:

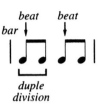

⑤ **Listening Questions**
#1 - How many big sections are in this piece?
#2 - Are any of them the same?
#3 - Using letters of the alphabet to match sections which are alike, what is the form of this piece in letters?

⑥ **Answers:**

#3 - ABA
#2 - Yes, the first and third
#1 - 3

Exercise #8

CD Track
9

① **Key: A major** (student may use open A and E strings, and fingers 1, 2, and 3 on A and E. The second finger should be placed touching the third finger as it is in the Twinkle Variations of Suzuki Book One.)

Advanced Finger Pattern: Use all strings described in the diagram. Note that open G string cannot be used, but can be replaced by a first finger, lowered into half position. Also notice that the third finger is raised on D and G strings. Third position may also be used on the E string with a fourth finger extending beyond into fourth position. This extended fourth finger should be played as a harmonic: The finger lightly touches the string but does not press it down to the fingerboard.

Clicks: 7

② **Basic Instructions:**
Using the finger pattern for A major (above) the student may play anything he wants. He cannot make a mistake since it is his own creation. The instructor should never interrupt the student once the playing has begun, (even if the student is using the wrong key or finger pattern).
Upon completion, compliment the student and repeat the exercise three to four times. If there is a confusion regarding the finger pattern, explain it again between repetitions.

Third Position with a Fourth Finger Harmonic Extension

③ **Advanced Instructions:**

Exercise #1: Listen carefully to the recording and try to identify the A section (or first section) every time it repeats. Create a melody or part of a melody for this A section and try to repeat it each time the A section recurs.

Exercise #2: Find a section that recurs other than the A section and create a melody or partial melody for it. Repeat the melody as often as the section repeats.

④ **About the Music:**

This piece is based on a combination of a Ragtime and Rock-n-Roll style rhythmic feel in a large ABA song form. In the recordings, as was traditional in Ragtime and is common in Rock-n-Roll, the performer uses the basic melodic and harmonic material provided and improvises upon it.

⑤ **Listening Questions:**

#1 - How many different sections are there in this piece?
#2 - How many times does each section repeat?
#3 - Using letters what is the form of this piece?

⑥ **Answers:**

ABCA DD ABCA - 3#
#2 - A section - 4 times, B, C and D sections - 2 times each.
#1 - 4

Exercise #9

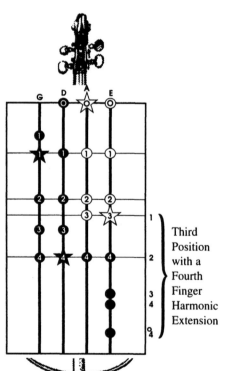

Third Position with a Fourth Finger Harmonic Extension

① **Key: A major** (student may use open A and E strings, and fingers 1, 2, and 3 on A and E. The second finger should be placed touching the third finger as it is in the Twinkle Variations of Suzuki Book One.)

Advanced Finger Pattern: Use all strings described in the diagram. Note that open G string cannot be used, but can be replaced by a first finger, lowered into half position. Also notice that the third finger is raised on D and G strings. Third position may also be used on the E string with a fourth finger extending beyond into fourth position. This extended fourth finger should be played as a harmonic: The finger lightly touches the string but does not press it down to the fingerboard.

Clicks: 4

② **Basic Instructions:**

Using the finger pattern for A major (above) the student may play anything he wants. He cannot make a mistake since it is his own creation. The instructor should never interrupt the student once the playing has begun, (even if the student is using the wrong key or finger pattern). Upon completion, compliment the student and repeat the exercise three to four times. If there is a confusion regarding the finger pattern, explain it again between repetitions.

③ **Advanced Instructions:**

Exercise #1: Think of your improvisation as a duet part to the melody in the upper voice of the piano. Create answering phrases in a similar style to the melody and try to place them in the spaces between the phrases.

Exercise #2: Improvise matching the melodic line rhythmically and leave spaces where they occur in the melody.

④ **About the Music:**

This piece was created as an improvisation in the classical style using an alberti bass as an accompaniment. The classical style refers to a period of time in which composers such as Beethoven, Mozart and Haydn worked. Their music best represents a style in which clarity, balance and objectivity was more important than the romantic ideals of exaggeration, unrest and subjectivity. The alberti bass refers to an accompaniment style which is based on chords which are broken into a single characteristic figure (i.e.:) and repeatedthroughout the piece. The improviser of this piece began with a motive (a small phrase of music which he then used to develop the entire piece. A motive works like the seed of a tree: The seed is planted and a tree grows from it, but only with the elements contained in the seed. For example, the seed of a maple tree can only grow a maple tree. In music, elements such as rhythm, decoration, pitch relationships, etc. all contribute to how a piece may develop. Listen to the piece again and try to hear the similarities and relationships to the opening measure throughout the piece.

⑤ **Questions:**
#1 - What is the purpose of the fast notes in the melody? Are they rhythmic?

⑥ **Answers:**

#1 - They decorate the melody. These notes are not strictly rhythmic, they are more free. They are referred to as grace notes, ornaments or decorations. In the past they were often improvised by the performer in concert. Try adding some ornaments of your own when you improvise.

Exercise #10

CD Track
11

① **Key: A major** (student may use open A and E strings, and fingers 1, 2, and 3 on A and E. The second finger should be placed touching the third finger as it is in the Twinkle Variations of Suzuki Book One.)

Advanced Finger Pattern: Use all strings described in the diagram. Note that open G string cannot be used, but can be replaced by a first finger, lowered into half position. Also notice that the third finger is raised on D and G strings. Third position may also be used on the E string with a fourth finger extending beyond into fourth position. This extended fourth finger should be played as a harmonic: The finger lightly touches the string but does not press it down to the fingerboard.

Clicks: 6

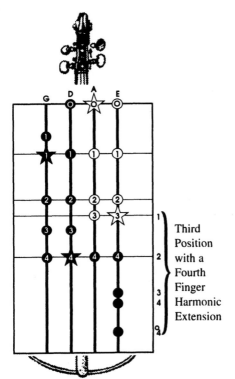

Third Position with a Fourth Finger Harmonic Extension

② **Basic Instructions:**
Using the finger pattern for A major (above) the student may play anything he wants. He cannot make a mistake since it is his own creation.
The instructor should never interrupt the student once the playing has begun (even if the student is using the wrong key or finger pattern). Upon completion, compliment the student and repeat the exercise three to four times. If there is a confusion regarding the finger pattern, explain it again between repetitions.

③ **Advanced Instructions**

Exercise #1 - Listen to the piece and try to imagine or sing a melody in the spaces. Do the exercise again but this time try to play whatever you sang or imagined.

Exercise #2 - Improvise with the melody but never play in the spaces.

Exercise #3 - Improvise with the melody but always play a different rhythm than the melody.

④ **About the Music:**

This piece, like number nine, was also improvised but this time in a more romantic style. While the romantic style places a greater emphasis on the emotional content, it still requires a great deal of structure to make it cohesive. This improvisation uses a motive introduced at the beginning, as well as a variation form to structure the piece. There are three variations which follow the introduction of the theme, the third of which develops into the climax of the piece. This variation is followed by a return to the original theme which is extended and ended by a coda section.

⑤ **Listening Questions:**

#1 - How many times can you find the notes of the first measure of the piece duplicated exactly?

⑥ **Answers:**

#1 - One time exactly and one time almost exactly following the climax or high point in the piece.

Exercise #11

① Key: D Pentatonic (The student may use 1 and 3 on A and E as well as open A and E strings. The fingers should be placed on the tapes as shown.)

Advanced Finger Pattern: The advanced finger pattern for this Key is 1 and 3 on A and E, 1 and 2 on D and G with no open G allowed. Open D, A and E are all allowed as well as 4th fingers. 2nd fingers are placed high as though next to 3rd fingers. See diagram for further clarity.

Clicks: 4

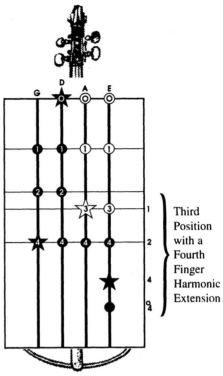

② Basic Instructions: Using the finger pattern for D pentatonic (above) the student may play anything he wants. He cannot make a mistake since it is his own creation. The instructor should never interrupt the student once the playing has begun, (even if the student is using the wrong key or finger pattern). Upon completion, compliment the student and repeat the exercise three to four times. If there is a confusion regarding the finger pattern, explain it again between repetitions.

③ Advanced Instructions:
Exercise #1 - Follow the recorded melodic phrases with an answer, imitating the rhythm but not the pitch. Play freely in the middle section.
Exercise #2 - Follow the recorded melodic phrases with an answer, but do not imitate the rhythm of them. Play a different rhythm in the middle section where there are only repeated chords.

④ About the Music:
This piece uses the Key of D Pentatonic. It has only five different pitches thus the name "Penta" (from the Greek meaning five). This scale occurs in nearly all ancient cultures as a first mode or scale.* Because of its simplicity, and the fact that no two notes are closer than a whole step apart (i.e. no two fingers touch), no dissonance occurs. The form is a simple ABA with the A section being in a question and answer form.

⑤ Listening Question:
#1 - How many different pitches are there in this piece?

⑥ Answers:
#1 - 5 - All others repeat at the octave. The names of the notes are D, E, F#, A and B. Open A for example, can be repeated an octave higher by placing 3 on E.

Exercise #12

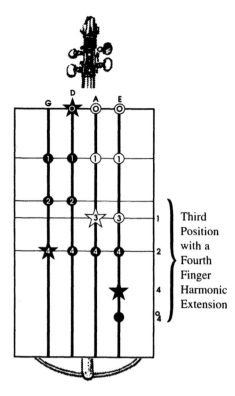

Third
Position
with a
Fourth
Finger
Harmonic
Extension

① **Key: D Pentatonic** (The student may use 1 and 3 on A and E as well as open A and E strings. The fingers should be placed on the tapes as shown.)

Advanced Finger Pattern: The advanced finger pattern for this Key is 1 and 3 on A and E, 1 and 2 on D and G with no open G allowed. Open D, A and E are all allowed as well as 4th fingers. 2nd fingers are placed high as though next to 3rd fingers. See diagram for further clarity.

Clicks: 4

② **Basic Instructions:** Using the finger pattern for D pentatonic (above) the student may play anything he wants. He cannot make a mistake since it is his own creation. The instructor should never interrupt the student once the playing has begun, (even if the student is using the wrong key or finger pattern). Upon completion, compliment the student and repeat the exercise three to four times. If there is a confusion regarding the finger pattern, explain it again between repetitions.

③ **Advanced Instructions:**
Exercise #1 - Listen carefully and identify the sections of the piece: There are two A sections a B section and a return to the A section. The A sections have a high melody with spaces between the phrases. The B section has a melody in the lowest part of the piano. Try to imagine answers to the melodic phrases in part A, and a melody over top of the one in part B. When you have done this try to play your ideas on your instrument.

④ **About the Music:**
This piece is in D pentatonic, structured by the form AABA. The B section contains a melody in the bass line, whereas the A section has the question and answer format of exercise #11.

⑤ **Listening Questions:**
#1 - What is unusual about the melody in this piece?

#2 - How are the melodies the same? How are they different?

⑥ **Answers:**

#1 - In the B section (or middle section) the melody appears in the lowest voice with the harmony above it.

#2 - The bass melody (low melody) and the soprano melody (high melody) have similar rhythms and similar melodic shapes. The actual pitches are different as are the harmonies supporting them. The soprano melody is supported by a basically major harmony, whereas the bass melody is supported by a minor harmony. Listen carefully to hear the difference.

Exercise #13

① Key: D Pentatonic (The student may use 1 and 3 on A and E as well as open A and E strings. The fingers should be placed on the tapes as shown.)

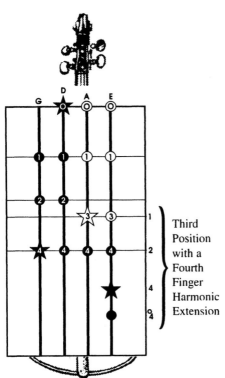

Third Position with a Fourth Finger Harmonic Extension

Advanced Finger Pattern: The advanced finger pattern for this Key is 1 and 3 on A and E, 1 and 2 on D and G with no open G allowed. Open D, A and E are all allowed as well as 4th fingers. 2nd fingers are placed high as though next to 3rd fingers. See diagram for further clarity.

Clicks: 4

② Basic Instructions: Using the finger pattern for D pentatonic (above) the student may play anything he wants. He cannot make a mistake since it is his own creation. The instructor should never interrupt the student once the playing has begun, (even if the student is using the wrong key or finger pattern). Upon completion, compliment the student and repeat the exercise three to four times. If there is a confusion regarding the finger pattern, explain it again between repetitions.

③ Advanced Instructions:

Exercise #1 - Answer the melodic questions in the first and last sections with imitative rhythms (but not pitches). Allow the melodic questions to overlap the end of your phrase.

Exercise #2 - Play as in Exercise #1 only answer with non-imitative rhythms this time.

Exercise #3 - Play throughout the piece: where there is melody play below it (i.e. D and A strings). Where there is no melody create your own on the A and E strings. (Note: You will need to use the advanced finger pattern for this key.)

④ About the Music:
This piece is in ABA form in the Key of D pentatonic. The A section is once again in a question/answer format. The B section is simply a rhythmic pattern which is repeated over and over while the pitches get higher and then lower again. Notice that although all the pitches of the pentatonic scale are being used simultaneously in the B section, there is still no dissonance or clashing of pitches.

⑤ Listening Questions:
#1 - What is the form of this piece using the letter system?

⑥ Answers:
#1 - ABA

CD Track
15

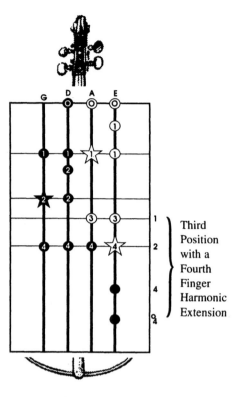

G D A E

Third Position with a Fourth Finger Harmonic Extension

① **Key: B minor blues scale** (The B minor blues scale uses the same finger pattern as the D pentatonic scale, 1 and 3 on A & E, with the following addition: The 1st finger can be lowered to the nut of the violin and then slid into the regular position as a decorative effect on both A & E. The first and last note played should be a B, 1st finger on the A string).

Advanced Finger Pattern: Use the advanced finger pattern for D pentatonic as before adding a slide from a low 2 to a high 2 on D and G as a decoration as well as the decorations described in the basic instructions above.

Clicks: 4

② **Basic Instructions:** Using the finger pattern for the B minor blues scale (above) the student may play anything he wants. He cannot make a mistake since it is his own creation. The instructor should never interrupt the student once the playing has begun, (even if the student is using the wrong key or finger pattern). Upon completion, compliment the student and repeat the exercise three to four times. If there is a confusion regarding the finger pattern, explain it again between repetitions.

③ **Advanced Instructions:**

Exercise #1 - Listen carefully to the harmonic pattern: You will notice that it repeats every 12 bars. You will also notice that a new part enters every 12 bars (Hint: In the beginning all of the new parts are percussion parts.) Play with the tape imitating the style and rhythm of the new parts as they come in.

Exercise #2 - Play with the tape changing rhythmic and melodic ideas every 12 bars without imitating the tape.

④ **About the Music:**

This piece is based on a traditional 12 bar blues pattern: I I I I IV IV I I V IV I I. The pattern of chords is repeated like "What's the Answer to My Question?" over and over with the parts above changing. In this case the upper parts enter one at a time every 12 bars. The parts are designed to work played at the same time and eventually they are. After all the parts are in, most drop out in a 'break' section which lasts 2 patterns. The final pattern brings all the parts back in to end the piece.

The blues style encompasses the use of a steady pulsating rhythm, a repeating harmonic pattern, and characteristic "blue" notes which are notes that fall between the normal notes of the scale. These notes are often approached or left by a portamento (or a slide).

⑤ **Listening Questions:**

#1 - How many times does the 12 bar blues pattern repeat?

#2 - How many different instruments (or groups of instruments) did you hear? What was the order of their appearance?

Exercise #15

① **Key: G Major** (Students may use all 4 strings in this key. 1 and 3 are placed on tapes (or in their natural positions) and 2nd finger is placed next to 1 on A and E, and next to 3 on D and G. This placement is often referred to as low 2 on A and E, high 2 on D and G. If the student has not learned this finger placement yet, you may either teach it to him here or skip the use of the 2nd finger altogether in this section until he is ready for it. Check with your teacher if you are not sure.)

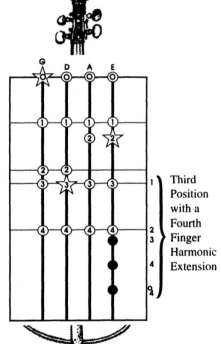

Third Position with a Fourth Finger Harmonic Extension

Advanced Finger Pattern: If the student is in book IV of the Suzuki repertoire and/or has begun use of higher positions he may use third position on E to obtain higher notes. See Diagram. 4th finger use is also optional.

Clicks: 4

② **Basic Instructions:** Using the finger pattern for G major (above) the student may play anything he wants. He cannot make a mistake since it is his own creation. The instructor should never interrupt the student once the playing has begun, (even if the student is using the wrong key or finger pattern). Upon completion, compliment the student and repeat the exercise three to four times. If there is a confusion regarding the finger pattern, explain it again between repetitions.

③ **Advanced Instructions:**

Exercise #1 - Sing the words "what's the answer to my question?" with the solo violin and then the cello at the beginning of the exercise.

Listen to this melody in the cello as you improvise over it.

Exercise #2 - Change your rhythm, articulation or dynamic with each new "what's the answer to my question?"

Exercise #3 - Listen carefully to the melody played by the violin. Try to play on a different string than the solo in the recording. You will have to change often.

Exercise #4 - Listen to the rhythms (the speed of the notes) of the solo violin part and try to match them. Do not match the notes themselves. Notice that the rhythms change with each "what's the answer to my question?"

Exercise #5 - Notice the holes or spaces in the solo violin part and try to fill them in with quicker notes.

Exercise #6 - Attempt to overlap rhythmic patterns by imitating the previous rhythm of the solo violin as it changes to a new one every "what's the answer to my question?" phrase.

④ **About the Music:**

This piece is exactly the same as exercise #1 on side A except that it has been transposed to the key of G. This key makes it easier for the beginning or intermediate student to use all four strings.

⑤ **Listening Questions:**

#1 - How many times can you find the melody "What's the answer to my question?" (See advanced instructions Exercise #1) "Who played it?"

#2 - The violin plays 9 different melodies over "What's the answer to my question?" then repeats them backwards. Which ones get left out the second time? Were any new ones added?

⑥ **Answers:**

#1 - 21
The first and last were played by the violin, the rest were played by the cello.

#2 - The eighth and ninth variation get left out the second time. (There is one new one at the end though a piece of it is at the very beginning of the song.)

52

Exercise #16

① **Key: G Major** (Students may use all four strings in this key. 1 and 3 are placed on tapes (or in their natural positions) and 2nd finger is placed next to 1 on A and E, and next to 3 on D and G. This placement is often referred to as low 2 on A and E, high 2 on D and G. If the student has not learned this finger placement yet, you may either teach it to him here or skip the use of the 2nd finger altogether in this section until he is ready for it. Check with your teacher if you are not sure.)

Advanced Finger Pattern: If the student is in book IV of the Suzuki repertoire and/or has begun use of higher positions he may use third position on E to obtain higher notes. See Diagram. 4th finger use is also optional.

Clicks: 6

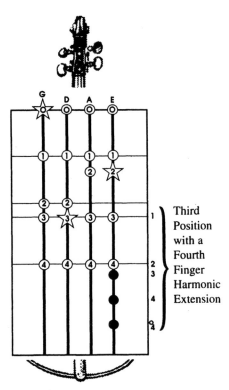

Third Position with a Fourth Finger Harmonic Extension

② **Basic Instructions:**
Using the finger pattern for G major (above) the student may play anything he wants. He cannot make a mistake since it is his own creation. The instructor should never interrupt the student once the playing has begun, (even if the student is using the wrong key or finger pattern). Upon completion, compliment the student and repeat the exercise three to four times. If there is a confusion regarding the finger pattern, explain it again between repetitions.

③ **Advanced Instructions:**
Exercise #1 - Listen for the "what's the answer to my question?" melody. You will find it in the cello part in this exercise, doubled by the piano. Listen to it as you improvise over it.

Exercise #2 - Listen to the "what's the answer to my question?" melody and change your rhythm, dynamic or articulation each time there is a repeat of the cello melody. How many different ways can you find to play your violin? Some suggestions: Pizzicato, violin upside down, bow on the bridge, bow on the fingerboard, bow upside down, bow bouncing etc.

Exercise #3 - Listen to the violins and try not to play the same notes. Try to play on a different string whenever possible.

Exercise #4 - Try to play in the spaces left by the longer held notes in the violins. Notice how the second violin often fills in the spaces left by the first violin in the first half of the piece. In the second half, the second violin drops out leaving more room for the improviser to fill in the spaces.

④ **About the Music:**
Like the first exercise, this one is also a passacaglia using the same bass line, only this time it's in the more traditional triple meter. The violin parts are written as a loose canon, meaning that the first violin plays a melody which is then played by the second violin while the first violin continues with a new part. Both violins play the same part but one starts 8 bars before the other. (Common examples of canons are the folk songs "Row, Row, Row Your Boat" or "Frere Jacques.") In the exercise, the canon is played once with two violins and is then heard only by the solo violin.

⑤ **Listening Questions:**
#1 - How many times did you hear "What's the answer to my question?" played by both the cello and piano?

#2 - Are all the phrases canonic? If not, which are not?

⑥ **Answers:**

(uᴉloᴉʌ ʇsɹᴉɟ ǝɥʇ ɟo ǝsɐɹɥd
ɥʇuᴉu puɐ ʇsɹᴉɟ ǝɥʇ ɹo) ǝɔǝᴉd ǝɥʇ ɟo ɟlɐɥ ʇsɹᴉɟ ǝɥʇ uᴉ ɔᴉuouɐɔ ʇou ǝɹɐ sǝsɐɹɥd ʇsɐl puɐ ʇsɹᴉɟ ǝɥ⊥ - oN - ᄅ#
Iᄅ - I#

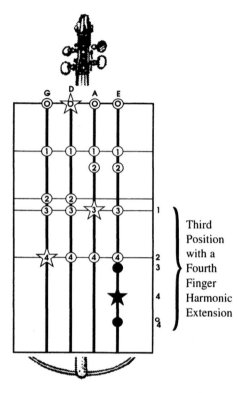

Exercise #17

CD Track 18

① **Key: Mode of D Mixolydian** (use the finger pattern for the key of G with the following addition: Begin and end the piece with the note D, 3rd finger on the A string or open D. See diagram).

Advanced Finger Pattern: Use the finger pattern for the key of G advanced, beginning and ending the piece on the note D.

Third Position with a Fourth Finger Harmonic Extension

Clicks: 4

② **Basic Instructions:** Using the finger pattern for the mode of D Mixolydian (above) the student may play anything he wants. He cannot make a mistake since it is his own creation. The instructor should never interrupt the student once the playing has begun, (even if the student is using the wrong key or finger pattern). Upon completion, compliment the student and repeat the exercise three to four times. If there is a confusion regarding the finger pattern, explain it again between repetitions.

③ **Advanced Instructions:**
Exercise #1 - Try to play on a different string than the violin on the tape. Avoid playing the same notes.

Exercise #2 - Try to create a countermelody to the violin staying above it most of the time.

④ **About the Music:**
This piece is in AABA form with the B section being a piano solo and the A section being a violin solo with piano accompaniment. Exercise #17 introduces a new concept in harmony: Harmony based on the same pitches as the key of G, but creating a whole new harmonic language based on where the tonic (or primary chord) of the piece is placed in the scale.

Diagram #1

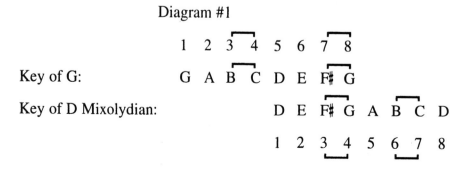

As you can see in Diagram #1, the pitches of the two keys are the same, but while the key of G starts on G, the key of D Mixolydian starts on D. Because of the different placement of the beginning of the scale there is a half step between the 6th and 7th scale steps in D Mixolydian, as opposed to the 7th and 8th scale steps in the key of G. This creates a completely different set of harmonies. However, due to the same set of pitches D mixolydian is said to be one of the modes of G Major. In the following exercises six of the modes of G will be introduced. In this way, the student can easily explore the harmonic and melodic characteristics of the modes without having to learn new finger patterns for any of them.

⑤ **Listening Questions:**

#1 - Why is it important to begin and end this piece on the pitch D?

#2 - Using letters, what is the form of this piece?

⑥ **Answers:**

#2 - AABA

#1 - It sounds like it should. The reason it does is because the main chord in this piece (called the tonic chord) has as its lowest note a D. The piano begins and ends with this chord. However, there are many other possibilities. Playing a different note than the tonic is not wrong and may indeed be a very beautiful melodic idea.

Exercise #18

CD Track 19

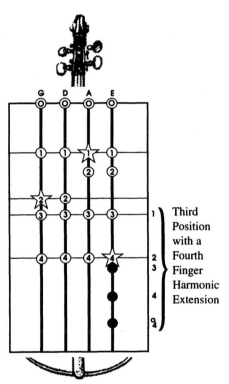

① **Key: Mode of B Phrygian** (Use the finger pattern for the key of G with the following addition: Begin and end the piece with the note B, first finger on A. See Diagram.)

Advanced Finger Pattern: Use the finger pattern for the Key of G advanced, beginning and ending the piece on the pitch B.

Clicks: 4

② **Basic Instructions:** Using the finger pattern for the mode of B Phrygian (above), the student may play anything he wants. He cannot make a mistake since it is his own creation. The instructor should never interrupt the student once the playing has begun, (even if the student is using the wrong key or finger pattern). Upon completion, compliment the student and repeat the exercise three to four times. If there is a confusion regarding the finger pattern, explain it again between repetitions.

③ **Advanced Instructions:**

Exercise #1 - Create a repeating rhythmic figure like the piano part and improvise an accompaniment rather than a melody.

Exercise #2 - Improvise an accompaniment during the violin solo and a countermelody during the cello solo.

④ **About the Music:**

The form of this trio for violin, cello and piano is ABCA. The new mode introduced here is B Phrygian. As in the mode of D Mixolydian, the character of the harmony changes dramatically due to the new placement of the tonic chord on B and the resulting change in the placement of half steps. See Diagram.

Diagram #2

	1	2	3	4	5	6	7	8
G Major scale:	G	A	B	C	D	E	F♯	G
B Phrygian scale:		B	C	D	E	F♯	G	A	B
		1	2	3	4	5	6	7	8

The B Phrygian scale has a minor sound with a lowered second and sixth scale step.

⑤ **Listening Questions:**

#1 - What is the form of this piece? What instruments play the different sections?

#2 - Why is it important to begin and end this piece on the pitch B?

⑥ **Answers:**

#1 - ABCA - the violin and piano play the A and B sections, the cello and piano play the C section.

#2 - It sounds like it should. The key or mode of B Phrygian has as its main (or tonic chord) a B minor chord, the lowest pitch of this chord being a B. The other two pitches of this chord, D or F♯, could be substituted for the B and would also work well in a melodic or secondary accompaniment part. Again, there are many other possible notes that would also be beautiful. There are no wrong solutions.

Exercise #19

① **Key: Mode of C Lydian** (use the finger pattern of the key of G with the following addition: Begin and end the exercise with the pitch C, third finger on the G string or low second finger on the A string. See Diagram).

Advanced Finger Pattern: Use the advanced finger pattern for the key of G, beginning and ending on the pitch C.

Clicks: 4

② **Basic Instructions:** Using the finger pattern for the mode of C Lydian (above), the student may play anything he wants. He cannot make a mistake since it is his own creation. The instructor should never interrupt the student once the playing has begun, (even if the student is using the wrong key or finger pattern). Upon completion, compliment the student and repeat the exercise three to four times. If there is a confusion regarding the finger pattern, explain it again between repetitions.

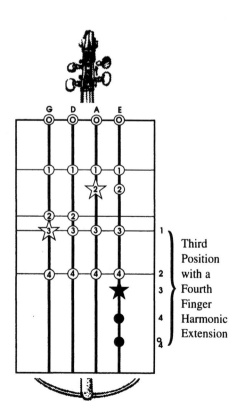

Third Position with a Fourth Finger Harmonic Extension

③ **Advanced Instructions:**

Exercise #1 - Listen carefully and you will hear the opening phrase return at the end. Create a countermelody to this phrase and try to remember it at the end when the phrase repeats. Sing or imagine it first, then play it.

④ **About the Music:**

This exercise is a simple piece that develops out of its opening theme, and then returns to it at the end. It is in the mode of C Lydian which falls on the fourth scale step of the Key of G. See Diagram:

Diagram #3

```
                        ┌─┐        ┌─┐
                1  2  3  4  5  6  7  8
                        ┌─┐        ┌─┐
Key of G Scale:    G  A  B  C  D  E  F♯ G

Mode of C Lydian:           C  D  E  F♯ G  A  B  C
                                              ┌─┐
                            1  2  3  4  5  6  7  8
                                     └─┘     └─┘
```

The mode of C Lydian has a major sound with a raised fourth scale step.

⑤ **Listening Questions:**

#1 - What characteristic is shared by this piece and Exercise #12?

#2 - What is the tonic or main chord of this piece?

⑥ **Answers:**

#2 - C Major. The main pitch of C lydian is C and the chord that forms above it is major.

#1 - The melody moves from the upper voice to the lower voice and back again.

Exercise #20

CD Track 21

① **Key: G Major** (Follow the diagram and begin and end on G.)

Advanced Finger Pattern: Follow the instruction for advanced key of G finger pattern and begin and end on G.

Clicks: 4

② **Basic Instructions:** Using the finger pattern for G major (above), the student may play anything he wants. He cannot make a mistake since it is his own creation. The instructor should never interrupt the student once the playing has begun, (even if the student is using the wrong key or finger pattern). Upon completion, compliment the student and repeat the exercise three to four times. If there is a confusion regarding the finger pattern, explain it again between repetitions.

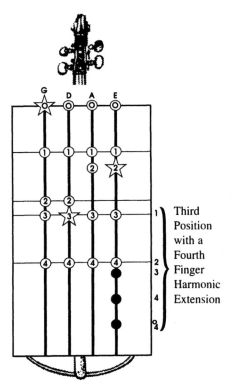

1 Third
Position
with a
2 Fourth
3 Finger
Harmonic
4 Extension

③ **Advanced Instructions:**

Exercise #1 - Listen to the style and rhythmic feel of each solo instrument as it enters. Try to imitate that feel after the instrument drops out.

④ **About the Music:**

This exercise consists of a simple four bar chord progression which repeats over and over. The melodies which come in and out are in a pop style and have a rhythmic feel which is referred to as "swing."

⑤ **Listening Questions:**

#1 - How many different chords are there in this piece?

#2 - Can you think of a famous pop song which uses this chord progression?

⑥ **Answers:**

#2 - "Heart and Soul."

#1 - 4

Exercise #21

CD Track 22

① **Key: E Natural Minor** (Use the finger pattern for the key of G with the following addition: Begin and end the piece with the note E, open E string or first finger on the D string.)

Advanced Finger Pattern: Follow the instructions for the advanced key of G finger pattern but begin and end on the pitch E.

Clicks: 3

② **Basic Instructions:** Using the finger pattern for E Natural Minor (above) the student may play anything he wants. He cannot make a mistake since it is his own creation. The instructor should never interrupt the student once the playing has begun, (even if the student is using the wrong key or finger pattern). Upon completion, compliment the student and repeat the exercise three to four times. If there is a confusion regarding the finger pattern, explain it again between repetitions.

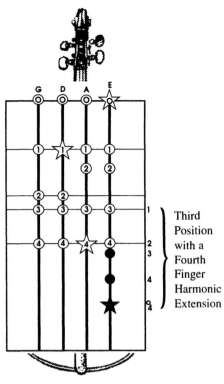

Third Position with a Fourth Finger Harmonic Extension

③ **Advanced Instructions:**
Exercise #1 - Listen carefully to the tape and identify the A sections: You should hear five of them. Imagine a phrase of countermelody to the A sections and try to sing it each time the A section returns. Repeat the exercise, this time playing the similar phrase for the A sections while improvising freely during the B and C sections.

④ **About the Music:**
This exercise is a slow waltz in rondo form. Rondo form is strictly speaking ABACABA, the A section recurring several times like a refrain. The mode of E Natural Minor is once again related to G Major by virtue of containing all the same pitches. In this case the new mode starts on the sixth scale step of G Major.

1	2	3	4	5	6	7	8

Key of G: G   A   B   C   D   E   F♯   G

Key of E Natural Minor: E   F♯   G   A   B   C   D   E

   1   2   3   4   5   6   7   8

Every major key has as its relative minor the mode which starts on the sixth scale step. This relationship was widely developed in the Baroque and Classical periods of music history.

⑤ **Listening Questions:**
#1 - What is the form of this piece?

#2 - What key does the B section sound like it's in? Does it move away from e minor?

⑥ **Answers:**
#2 - Key of G. It moves away from E Natural Minor, but returns to it when the A section returns.

#1 - ABACABA (also known as rondo form)

Exercise #22

① **Key: Mode of C Lydian** (use the finger pattern of the key of G with the following addition: Begin and end the exercise with the pitch C, third finger on the G string or low second finger on the A string. See Diagram).

Advanced Finger Pattern: Use the advanced finger pattern for the key of G, beginning and ending on the pitch C.

Clicks: 4

② **Basic Instructions:** Using the finger pattern for the mode of C Lydian (above), the student may play anything he wants. He cannot make a mistake since it is his own creation. The instructor should never interrupt the student once the playing has begun, (even if the student is using the wrong key or finger pattern). Upon completion, compliment the student and repeat the exercise three to four times. If there is a confusion regarding the finger pattern, explain it again between repetitions.

Third Position with a Fourth Finger Harmonic Extension

③ **Advanced Instructions:**

Exercise #1: Listen carefully to the piece. You will hear an ABA form in which the A section is in 6/8 and the B section is in 2/4. 6/8 is a meter in which the main pulse or beat is divided into groups of three, whereas 2/4 is a meter in which the pulse or beat is divided into groups of two. Play imitating the meter of each section.

Exercise #2 - Follow the instructions for exercise #1 except this time create a free rhythm that can work with both the A and B sections.

④ **About the Music:**

This piece is an ABA form in the mode of C Lydian (which was introduced in exercise #19). It employs an interesting device called a Rhythmic Modulation. The modulation occurs in the transitional music from A to B and from B to A. The 6/8 triplet division of A gradually works its way into the 2/4 duple division of B and then reverses itself. It does this by keeping the beat the same while using both the triplet and the duple division for a few bars until the new rhythm has been established.

⑤ **Listening Questions:**
#1 - What is the form of this piece?

⑥ **Answers:**

#1 - A B A (coda) - the little section on the end which is similar to A and serves to end the piece is called a coda.

Exercise #23

CD Track
24

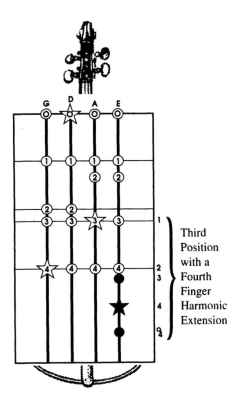

① **Key: Mode of D Mixolydian** (use the finger pattern for the key of G with the following addition: Begin and end the piece with the note D, 3rd finger on the A string or open D. See diagram).

Advanced Finger Pattern: Use the finger pattern for the key of G advanced, beginning and ending the piece on the note D.

Clicks: 6

② **Basic Instructions:** Using the finger pattern for the mode of D Mixolydian (above), the student may play anything he wants. He cannot make a mistake since it is his own creation. The instructor should never interrupt the student once the playing has begun, (even if the student is using the wrong key or finger pattern). Upon completion, compliment the student and repeat the exercise three to four times. If there is a confusion regarding the finger pattern, explain it again between repetitions.

③ **Advanced Instructions:**

Exercise #1 - Create a countermelody on the lower strings of the violin primarily using the D and G strings.

Exercise #2 - This exercise is in an ABA form. The B section is in a different key. Be very aware of the change of key and change your pitches according to what you hear as important to the new key.

Exercise #3 - Create a melody or part of a melody for the A section and return to it when the A section returns.

④ **About the Music:**

This piece is an ABA form in the key of D Mixolydian. It has an interesting feature in that it modulates harmonically to a different key in the B section. Because the key it modulates to is e minor, another one of the modes of G, the student does not need to change his finger pattern at all. While the notes don't change, the tonal center or tonic chord does. The shift occurs through a change in function of shared chords and an emphasis on the new tonal center. If you listen carefully you will hear the shared chords preceding the B section and in the return to the A section.

⑤ **Listening Questions:**

#1 - What is the form of this piece?

#2 - What key does it modulate to in the B section? How can you tell?

⑥ **Answers:**

#1 - ABA

#2 - E natural minor: The main pitch both in the lowest and highest voice is E, and the chord is minor. It is natural because all of the pitches are unaltered from its relative major key of G.

Exercise #24

CD Track 25

① **Key: G Major** (Follow the diagram and begin and end on G.)

Advanced Finger Pattern: If the student is in book IV of the Suzuki repertoire and/or has begun use of higher positions he may use third position on E to obtain higher notes. See Diagram. 4th finger use is also optional. Begin and end on G.

Clicks: 4

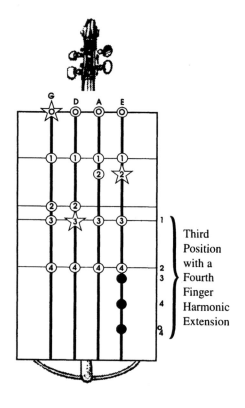

Third Position with a Fourth Finger Harmonic Extension

② **Basic Instructions:** Using the finger pattern for G major (above) the student may play anything he wants. He cannot make a mistake since it is his own creation. The instructor should never interrupt the student once the playing has begun, (even if the student is using the wrong key or finger pattern). Upon completion, compliment the student and repeat the exercise three to four times. If there is a confusion regarding the finger pattern, explain it again between repetitions.

③ **Advanced Instructions:**
Exercise #1: Listen to the violin, then play while it rests. Do not imitate its rhythm.

Exercise #2: Listen to the violin, then play while it rests. Imitate the preceding rhythm. In the final refrain play with the piano and violin.

Exercise #3: Play with the violin and/or the piano using two strings at a time. This is called using double stops. You may place fingers on one or both strings or neither as you please.

Exercise #4: During the violin parts play an accompaniment figure (i.e. a simple repeated rhythm below the violin solo or a part played pizzicato), then play a melodic figure while it rests. At the end fill in the final rest with 16th notes.

④ **About the Music:**
This piece is in the rhythmic style of a hoe-down, an early American dance often played on a fiddle (a violin played in a different manner and position). It follows an ABACDC form with each section being repeated harmonically following the violin melody with the exception of the final C which is played with both parts in the piano and then with the violin.

⑤ **Listening Questions:**
#1 - What is the form of this piece?

#2 - Where is the melody in the final two C sections?

#3 - Where do the final notes come from?

⑥ **Answers:**

#3 - The final notes come from the tail end of the C section.

#2 - The melody in the first C section is in the piano. The melody in the second C section is in the violin.

#1 - Aa Bb Aa Cc Dd CC

The capital letters represent the melody and harmony together, the small letters represent the harmony by itself.

Exercise #25

① **Key: Mode of A Dorian** (Use the finger pattern for the key of G Major with the following addition: Begin and end the piece on the pitch A. A can be found as first finger on the G string, open A string or third finger on the E string. See diagram.)

Advanced Finger Pattern: Follow the advanced finger pattern for the key of G, but begin and end the piece on the pitch A.

Clicks: 4

② **Basic Instructions:** Using the finger pattern for the mode of A Dorian (above) the student may play anything he wants. He cannot make a mistake since it is his own creation. The instructor should never interrupt the student once the playing has begun, (even if the student is using the wrong key or finger pattern). Upon completion, compliment the student and repeat the exercise three to four times. If there is a confusion regarding the finger pattern, explain it again between repetitions.

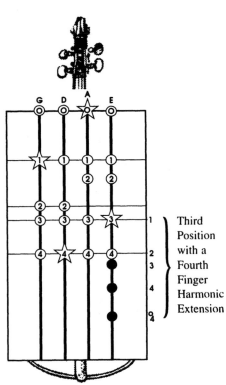

③ **Advanced Instructions:**
Exercise #1 - Play only on the D, A, and E strings, creating your own melody over the piano and violin countermelody.

Exercise #2 - Create a melody or phrase for the beginning of the A section and return to it when A repeats.

④ **About the Music:**
This piece is in A Dorian, the second mode of G. Because the third pitch in the scale forms a half step to the second pitch this mode has a minor quality, the lowered third scale step being the characteristic sound of a minor chord.

Diagram #5

	1	2	3	4	5	6	7	8
Key of G Major:	G	A	B	C	D	E	F♯	G
Mode of A Dorian:		A	B	C	D	E	F♯	G	A

The form of this piece is ABA with each section being repeated either adding or deleting the violin part.

⑤ **Listening Questions:**
#1 - What is the form of this piece? Try using capital and small letters.

#2 - Is A Dorian primarily a major or minor sounding mode? (Hint: Listen to the A sections to answer this question.)

#3 - What two pitches or chords does the B section center around? Are they major or minor chords?

⑥ **Answers:**
#3 - C and D Major.

#2 - Minor

#1 - a B B♭ a B a A

63

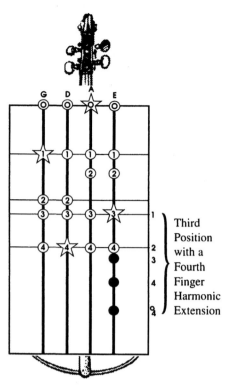

Exercise #26

① **Key: Mode of A Dorian** (Use the finger pattern for the key of G Major with the following addition: Begin and end the piece on the pitch A. A can be found as first finger on the G string, open A string or third finger on the E string. (See diagram.)

Advanced Finger Pattern: Follow the advanced finger pattern for the key of G, but begin and end the piece on the pitch A.

Clicks: 4

② **Basic Instructions:** Using the finger pattern for the mode of A Dorian (above), the student may play anything he wants. He cannot make a mistake since it is his own creation. The instructor should never interrupt the student once the playing has begun, (even if the student is using the wrong key or finger pattern). Upon completion, compliment the student and repeat the exercise three to four times. If there is a confusion regarding the finger pattern, explain it again between repetitions.

③ **Advanced Instructions:**
Exercise #1 - Listen carefully and you will hear a harmonic pattern which repeats over and over. Each time it repeats change one or more of the following things: Rhythmic pattern, articulation, dynamic, bowing, etc. How many different ways can you discover to vary your style of playing?

④ **About the Music:**
This piece, in the style of a march-like dance, is in the mode of A Dorian. It is essentially just a repeated section of music which contrasts only with dynamics. This allows the student to create his own set of variations over top of the harmony.

⑤ **Listening Questions:**
#1 - How many times does the harmonic pattern repeat?

#2 - Using 'F' for the loud sections and 'P' for the soft sections can you write a form based on dynamics? (Note: F stands for forte or big, P stands for piano or soft)

⑥ **Answers:**
F F P F P F P P F P F - 2#

#1 - 10

Exercise #27

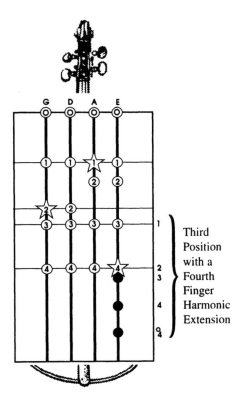

① **Key: Mode of B Phrygian** (Use the finger pattern for the key of G with the following addition: Begin and end the piece with the note B, first finger on A. See diagram.)

Advanced Finger Pattern: Use the finger pattern for the key of G advanced, beginning and ending the piece on the pitch B.

Clicks: 3

② **Basic Instructions:** Using the finger pattern for the mode of B Phrygian (above), the student may play anything he wants. He cannot make a mistake since it is his own creation. The instructor should never interrupt the student once the playing has begun, (even if the student is using the wrong key or finger pattern). Upon completion, compliment the student and repeat the exercise three to four times. If there is a confusion regarding the finger pattern, explain it again between repetitions.

③ **Advanced Instructions:**
Exercise #1: Create a rhythm which works well against the solo violin part and repeat it as an accompaniment figure. In the middle section play a melody in a free rhythmic style, and when the violin solo returns switch back to your original accompaniment figure.

④ **About the Music:**
This little piece is in the style of a Spanish dance in B Phrygian. When the violin drops out, the A section is repeated harmonically, the pianist improvising using the same chord progression. The form is therefore A a A.

⑤ **Listening Questions:**
#1 - What is the form of this piece? (Hint: Could you sing the violin part over the middle section?)

⑥ **Answers:**
#1 - A a A. The middle section is a harmonic repeat of the first and last sections.

Exercise #28

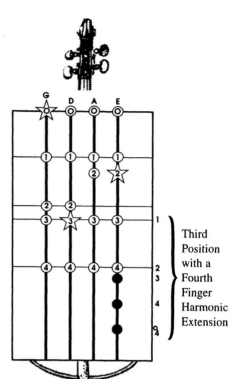

Third Position with a Fourth Finger Harmonic Extension

① **Key: G Major** (Follow the diagram and begin and end on G.)

Advanced Finger Pattern: If the student is in book IV of the Suzuki repertoire and/or has begun use of higher positions he may use third position on E to obtain higher notes. See Diagram. 4th finger use is also optional. Begin and end on the pitch G.

Clicks: 6

② **Basic Instructions:** Using the finger pattern for G major (above), the student may play anything he wants. He cannot make a mistake since it is his own creation. The instructor should never interrupt the student once the playing has begun, (even if the student is using the wrong key or finger pattern). Upon completion, compliment the student and repeat the exercise three to four times. If there is a confusion regarding the finger pattern, explain it again between repetitions.

③ **Advanced Instructions:**
Exercise #1: Create a countermelody with the A section. Try to play it every time the A part returns.

Exercise #2: Create a countermelody with the B section. Try to play it every time the B section returns. (Note that the B section returns without a melody in the second half.)

Exercise #3: Create a countermelody with the C section. Try to play it every time the C section returns. (Note that the C section only returns once and without the melody.)

Exercise #4: Combine exercises 1, 2 and 3.

④ **About the Music:**
This final piece is a G major rondo (an ABACABA form) which repeats the B and C sections without melody the second time. Like exercise #27, these second B and C sections were improvised based on the harmonic progression previously created for these sections.

⑤ **Listening Questions:**
#1 - What is the form of this exercise? (Use Capital and small letters.)

#2 - What is the name of this form?

⑥ **Answers:**

#2 - Rondo form: In this case the entire rondo is repeated.

#1 - A B A C A B A A b A c A b A

PART IV

BEYOND PRACTICE

THE HIGHER GOALS OF C.A.D.
TRUTH AND BEAUTY

I believe, as have many before me, that great creative ability is born of the search for truth and beauty. In our search to understand our world, and in our need to create a better one, lie the roots of all genius and all of the growth and development of mankind. Throughout history, those men and women with the greatest need to understand and communicate truth and beauty were those who were responsible for the most important and lasting achievements.

It is with this in mind that I address the importance of the element of need. How we instill in the students a need for truth and beauty is equally important to every other element in this method.

First of all, it is important to recognize that every child is born with needs and is therefore creative from birth. It is the infant's need to survive that first begins the development of his creative ability. As his physical and emotional needs grow, so does his ability to communicate those needs. Every new communication is creative and is applauded with love and praise, and results in the satisfaction of needs. It is very early in life that most children begin their search for the high aesthetic goals of truth and beauty, and also at the same time begin to communicate their aesthetic ideas to others. Usually they begin by communicating to their parents. This is the crucial time at which the child's creative ability may be either encouraged or destroyed.

Again the myths of creative genius are responsible for much of the destruction. People fail to realize that the first artistic or aesthetic communications, like other first communications, are usually not beautiful or great. But, like the first word, the first aesthetic communications must be applauded and praised with love and pride by the people who mean the most to the child. This acknowledgment is not a false one; it is the acknowledgment of the beginning of possibly the most important search of the child's life: The search for truth and beauty.

This search is characterized by choices by the student of right or wrong, good or bad, beautiful or ugly. Through choices of sound, the student is communicating his highest aesthetic abilities of the moment.

The search is a difficult one and must be encouraged. Again, the force of positive is far greater than the force of negative. Praise and love are unequaled forms of encouragement. Recognition of the greatness of what each child is accomplishing is extremely important. Expressiveness and beauty of sound may be encouraged by a few simple words. Most likely the student, having been rewarded for his attempt, will be more than willing to try even harder the next time.

Expressions may sometimes seem harsh or ugly. If this occurs, remember that the search may also be for truth. The student is expressing feelings he honestly has. It is important not to negatively criticize these expressions. Expressing interest in the student's endeavor, or attempting to understand through discussion, are valid ways of encouraging the student. Remember the student may not understand his own expression and it is not always necessary for him to understand it.

Truth may not always be beautiful, but there is always beauty in the expression of truth. Sincerity of expression is always the goal.

IN RETROSPECT

Our age has been called the "age of consciousness," with good reason. We concentrate most of our learning on logic and reason, and very little on creativity. However, any advancement in art, science, philosophy, medicine, etc., is through a combination of great intelligence and great creative ability. Indeed, "genius" is defined as "great mental capacity and inventive ability," and it is genius that keeps us moving forward on a path of greater humanity.

Obviously we can't all be geniuses, but I believe that geniuses are developed through their own deeply felt needs. The more we can create these needs in our children, the more like geniuses they will become and the greater our world will be as a result of their greater humanity.

It surprised me at first that children loved to come to Creative Ability Development class, and that after nine years, most of my first class has stayed together in spite of changing life-styles and commitments; but now I see that Creative Ability Development has satisfied a need that was unfulfilled elsewhere. Perhaps all they needed was an outlet for all the creativity that was growing inside themselves and they found it in a place where they could share it with each other without criticism.

The children in this class are very good friends and care about each other in a way that I have rarely seen in a classroom. They are respectful, supportive and generous with each other. If they are an example of what the world would be like if all children were encouraged to be creative, the world would be a better place to live.

In retrospect, it is not surprising that these children should be as they are. Creativity is the opposite of destructiveness: When one becomes creative and creates things, one has a greater understanding of, and respect for, the work and sensitivity that goes into new creations. Therefore, one has no desire to destroy or see anyone else destroy a creation.

Perhaps, then the equation is simple:

> To teach them, encourage them, and allow them to fulfill their own natural needs in creative ways;
>
> To encourage them to be sincere in their expression (which is the search for truth);
>
> To encourage them to be their best (which is the search for beauty);
>
> And to teach them to be always open to, and to have respect for, the ideas of others.
> (Creativity is built on creativity: Each new idea grows from an old one.)

If we can learn to teach our children by this equation, we may see them grow to be like geniuses in their manner of thought and expression, and as a result, we may also see them grow to be greater human beings.